MEETING MONROE

CONVERSATIONS WITH A MAN WHO CAME TO EARTH

KINGSLEY L. DENNIS

BEAUTIFUL TRAITOR BOOKS

Copyright © 2013, 2016 by Kingsley L. Dennis

All rights reserved. No part of this work may be reproduced or transmitted in any form or by any means, electronic or mechanical, including photocopying and recording, or by any information storage or retrieval system without the prior written permission of Beautiful Traitor Books.

Published by Beautiful Traitor Books –
http://www.beautifultraitorbooks.com/

Any person who does any unauthorized act in relation to this publication may be liable to criminal prosecution and civil claims for damages. The author has asserted his right to be identified as the author of this work in accordance with the Copyright, Design and Patents Act 1988.

ISBN-13: 978-0-9954817-0-1 (paperback)

First published: November 2013

Revised edition: July 2016

Cover Concept: Kingsley L Dennis
Cover Design: Ibolya Kapta

Copyright 2016 by Beautiful Traitor Books. All rights reserved.
info@beautifultraitorbooks.com

Kingsley L Dennis, PhD, is an author and researcher. He currently lives in Andalusia, Spain.

He can be contacted at his personal website: www.kingsleydennis.com

By the same author

The Foundation: The Enigma of a Community

The Citadel: A Mystery at the Heart of Civilization

The Phoenix Generation: A New Era of Connection, Compassion, and Consciousness

Mundus Grundy: Trouble in Grundusland

Dawn of the Akashic Age: New Consciousness, Quantum Resonance, and the Future of the World (co-authored with Ervin Laszlo)

Breaking the Spell: An Exploration of Human Perception

New Revolutions for a Small Planet

The Struggle for Your Mind: Conscious Evolution & The Battle to Control How We Think

The New Science & Spirituality Reader (co-edited with Ervin Laszlo)

New Consciousness for a New World

After the Car (co-authored with John Urry)

For Strace
~ the old trout ~

&

To Bluebell
~ for those many questions dancing
on the tip of her tongue ~

A Teacher promised a disciple that he would reveal something much more important than was to be found in all the scriptures. When the disciple, being very impatient, asked the Teacher yet again to keep his promise, the Teacher said:
'Go outside into the rain, and stand with your arms open and your head raised to the sky.'
The next day, the disciple returned to the Teacher and informed him:
'I took your advice and I was soaked to the bone...I felt a perfect fool.'
'Well', replied the Teacher, 'for the first day that is quite a revelation, is it not?'

'Someone engaged in self-study should not have a fool for a teacher'

Anon

A NOTE FROM THE AUTHOR...7

INTRODUCTION 9

MEETING ONE 12

MEETING TWO 26

MEETING THREE 59

MEETING FOUR..79

MEETING FIVE 100

MEETING SIX 121

MEETING SEVEN...140

MEETING EIGHT 145

MEETING NINE 166

AFTERWORD...187

A NOTE FROM THE AUTHOR

I have finally decided to self-publish this book a year after it was first completed. The date on the introduction clearly states October 2012. I now allow this book to enter the public slipstream from November 2013. The delay was not intentional. This book of conversations dictated everything.

At one point I was in dialogue with the editor of a traditional mainstream publisher who showed interest in acquiring the book. There was talk of title changes in order to 'flash up' the book as 'Meeting Monroe' was deemed…well…just too ordinary! In the end, the book stayed tucked away; not wishing to be dressed up other than it is. The whole point is that this book is exactly what it is…and was meant to be published, in whatever way, in exactly the way it was delivered – nothing more, nothing less. It stands as a testament to its words, its energy, and the way it was delivered to me – in the most ordinary circumstances one could imagine!

INTRODUCTION

It is difficult to clearly express what happened to me over the period of several weeks in the spring of 2012. It was both an intense and a surreal experience. Even thinking about it now has me at a loss to give any credible explanation. It is probably best that I don't try to define or categorize what, in effect, was a series of startling and profound encounters. I have a feeling deep within that my meeting with the 'person' I came to know as Monroe was not an accident. Such encounters in life are rarely accidents; they are placed upon our paths for us to make the best from them – and to learn what they have to offer us. I also have a firm sense that whilst the experience was for me alone, the message was to be a shared one. That is why I have decided to write this book.

What is related in the following pages may seem unbelievable, even fanciful. Perhaps that is the whole point: it is not about belief. If it's one thing that Monroe has taught me it's that we are all blinded by our false systems of thought: beliefs, assumptions, opinions, etc. We create our own barriers to understanding, and we reinforce these limitations throughout our lives. I have come to understand that humanity is on the cusp of a remarkable stage in our evolutionary journey. As Monroe stressed to me on several occasions during our talks - we did not come this far for nothing.

The encounters take place in a small town located in the Sierra de Grazalema Natural Park in Andalusia, southern Spain. It is about forty kilometers from where I currently live, in the province of Cadiz. I do not wish to say much more at this stage. I only wish to open the door onto what, for me, were an incredible series of encounters and conversations. Monroe suggested that I record our conversations, which I did using a small digital voice recorder. The rest of the descriptive ambiance is my artistic license, drawn from a memory rich in the nuances of Monroe's behaviorisms and quirks. These I felt, and still do feel, were deliberately and very consciously coordinated, as if to put on a carefully crafted show. What follows are a series of encounters and conversations that I wrote in retrospect. I also took notes afterwards where I collected my mental pictures, my feelings, reactions, and my own thoughts. These were then interspersed throughout the text in the places where I felt were either accurate or appropriate. I have attempted to write of these encounters as if writing a novel, so that I can embellish the narrative where lacking (or missing), and to provide a sense of linearity. After all, the medium of speculative fiction may be the best channel for offering these conversations. That way, I am not insisting on the truth or the actuality of what happened. It's the truth even if it never happened anyway. What more can I say?

October 2012

MEETING ONE

I had driven to the small town of Benamahoma to park the car as there was a short walking route I wanted to take between Benamahoma and El Bosque. It was a pleasant track that followed the river and passed under the shade of the forest. On a gentle walk it would take 90 minutes each way. It was a walk I had taken several times before, and it was my preference to leave the car at Benamahoma, do the round trip, and have lunch at one of the local restaurants I knew that served excellent local food. A three-hour walk would usually be enough to create a decent appetite in me. Also, Benamahoma is known for its excellent local honey; something I usually took advantage of before leaving. Both Benamahoma and El Bosque are small white towns situated at the edge of the picturesque Sierra de Grazalema Natural Park. It was

March, 2012, and the spring had come early to Andalusia. The weeks had been kind to us with glorious sunshine and rising temperatures. Many of the flowers were blooming early, and people were preparing their vegetable gardens to begin planting the spring-summer crops of tomatoes, cucumbers, peppers, zucchinis, melons, and the rest. The soil was dry because we had had little rain over the winter. Neighbors had told me that after the previous several years of very wet winters, where we had witnessed a lot of flooding, we were now entering a dry cycle for the next couple of years.

With the early spring in my mind and in my step I entered the forest path to take me to El Bosque. I had deliberately chosen a week day so that there would be few people, and fewer families, crowding the narrow path as it curved following the river. Almost undisturbed I walked through the shadows of trees, occasionally hit by a stray ray of sunlight streaking through, and listened to the changing rhythms of the water. After a pleasant walk to El Bosque I took a cold beer at a small bar beside the river entrance, then made my way back to Benamahoma. My thoughts were elsewhere and everywhere, as was normal when I was rambling and roaming. As I approached the end of the walk my stomach turned its thoughts, and sounds, toward food and I visualized the local restaurant where I usually ate a pleasant lunch. To get to the restaurant I had to walk up a hill that was another ten minutes, and which wound past several houses perched on the slope of this mountain town. I casually meandered along the road and up the hill, looking beyond at the clear mountain vistas that rose up as rocky pinnacles piercing the blue Andalusian sky. I didn't see the man until I was almost upon him; I nearly stumbled into his rigid, upright body.

'Oh, perdón,' I said, in surprise. The man, who appeared to be in his early sixties, said nothing, only stared directly at me for a few unsettling moments. I thought that perhaps he was as surprised as me to have an English man almost walking into him; or perhaps he didn't think I understood any Spanish. In these few split seconds I managed a smile and a 'Buenos dias,' and turned to move on. Yet before my first step had made contact with the ground the man had begun to chuckle, showing a near-perfect set of strong white teeth, and in perfect English said 'Are you sure you know where you're going?'

'Errgh, yes,' I managed to say even more surprised; 'I'm heading for lunch at the restaurant at the top here.'

'Ah yes, by the fountain; I know it. It's a good place to eat. Yet they always have the same old food. I bet you'd rather try some different kinds of food from time to time?'

'Well,' I said smiling now at what appeared to be an affable English gentleman, 'I quite like the food there. Have you tried it?' At which point the man began to turn and continue walking up the hill.

Naturally, I followed, since it felt we were somehow in conversation, and anyhow I was going in that direction.

'Yes, I have; but I much prefer my own light lunches - and selective company too. Would you say you are a bit of a daydreamer?' the man asked as I walked beside him yet half a foot behind.

'Well, I don't know. I'm not sure really' I replied.

'I think perhaps you are,' he said smiling. 'That's okay though; everybody here seems to be dreaming! Yet some dream deeper than others. Do you know what we sometimes have to do for those who are only dreaming a little?' The man looked at me with a wry smile. I had no idea where the conversation was going or whether he was joking with me. The whole encounter seemed somewhat playful to me; and so in the sun of the day I played along with a light tone.

'No,' I said, 'what do you do?'

'Well, we pluck them out of course!' and he laughed. Stopping at the gate to a house that sloped down from the road of the hill he turned his gaze upwards and nodded. 'That's an eagle you can see up there; it has a nest on a mountain ridge like many other eagles. You can see them gliding on the air currents, their eyes focused below for movement. Eagles have sharp eyes. Have you ever wondered what humans look like from an eagle's perspective?'

'No,' I answered truthfully. Again, the man nodded; then fixed me with a soft smile.

'Tell me young man; is it your fate today to eat your usual lunch of wild boar with a glass of red wine, or is it to try something new – some different kind of food?' said the man. I really didn't know what to say. I had no clue what 'different food' he was referring to. Yet I found it pleasant to be speaking with this older English man, for it had been a while since I had had the opportunity to converse in English. I felt I was in need of a decent chat in my own mother tongue; and this guy seemed to have a reserved quirky side.

'Well, I'm open' I replied.

'Good, then follow me. Just imagine that I have a 'Follow Me' sign written on my back – that should make it easier!' chuckled the man as he strolled down the path toward a normal looking white-bricked Andalusian house. I closed the gate behind me and, as instructed, followed the imaginary sign on his back.

I sat down as indicated at a wooden table on the patio that had already been laid. Upon it were several small dishes of different cheeses; some Spanish cured ham; freshly cut local bread; and several other dishes of what appeared to be jam types. The man came and placed a chilled jug of water in the middle of the table and continued to pour. As I said, he appeared to be around his early sixties although it was difficult to be exact as his hair was whitish rather than grey, and his face had a youthful look albeit old of his years. And despite having a quirky sense to his facial features when one looked casually at his face it was inoffensively nondescript. There was an air of normality about the man which at times disappeared completely when, it seemed, he wished to override this. When I was just about to ask him his name he handed me a glass of water, and introduced himself as Monroe.

'There are different variations of my name that you could call me, yet Monroe is what works best,' and being English he gave me his hand to shake. And being English myself I gave it a firm shake and introduced myself; a bit too formally I thought.

'Unusual name' said Monroe. 'Has it helped you in life? I suppose it has.' He then gestured for me to eat.

'I'm not sure' I replied truthfully. 'When I was a young boy I didn't care much for my name; I guess it's the same with many. But then I came to like it; and somehow I feel it has helped. Names have a function.' I remembered that I wasn't sure exactly what I meant after I had said that final phrase – what kind of function did I mean? I had a niggling sensation that in Monroe's presence I was mimicking being more philosophical than I probably was, or thought I was. At first Monroe did not reply, but carefully placed some cheese onto the bread and slowly brought it up to his mouth, almost ceremoniously I thought. I selected some bread and Spanish ham and continued to eat.

'Names do indeed serve a function, as do particular words. Well, words are only vibrations, and they get picked up in your reality accordingly. Now, how do you find the cheese? It comes from a local village; there's both sheep and goat's cheese. I think you'll find the extra-cured sheep's cheese is a treat. How do you like living in Andalusia?'

'It's ideal for where I need to be right now' I said. 'I'm not sure how long I will be here, or whether I'll need to move again. But for now it's working.'

'Yes,' nodded Monroe, 'one must follow their instincts, and their needs. Places are contexts, they have a function for particular people at certain times, and these variants can and do alter. Energy falls at specific places in lesser or greater quantities according to context, and other matters.'

'Such as the layout of the geographical region?' I asked.

'On a lower level, yes. Yet everything is interconnected, interwoven with everything else. The cause and effect that you observe around you is a secondary, or even tertiary, manifestation. There is a lot going on at the moment. People need to keep their sense of balance and to be grounded.'

'Yes, I agree. The world is changing fast, especially in this transition window; and many of the world systems are crazy because they're stuck in wrong thinking. So I guess in some ways being in Andalusia is useful in that it shields you from some of the excesses going on in the world. And people here seem less distracted. Global events don't seem so global here, and locals don't talk much about this' I replied. I could sense that Monroe was an intelligent man, yet still remaining cautious in what he spoke.

'Perhaps not – but *you* talk about it, don't you?' Monroe said with a raised finger half-pointed directly at me.

'Well, it's what I'm interested in' I said, somewhat underplaying the depth of my interest.

'And you want answers too, yes?'

'Don't we all want answers?' As soon as I had said this I knew it was a blasé, evasive response. I immediately felt a little embarrassed at my standard, conditioned answer that didn't mean anything to either of us. Monroe just smiled and looked out over the view toward the mountains and the road that meandered in the distance. 'Not everyone is wishing for answers. Some are seeking, yet don't know how to ask the right questions yet. Others are not prepared to accept or understand the answers. And the majority, I'm afraid to say, don't really care. They have *their* world, and that is exactly where they are content to stay.' After saying this Monroe fell silent. A long pause gripped the table. I was content to eat in silence, trying to enjoy the same view that Monroe had been scanning a little before. For several minutes the both of us sat and ate in silence, enjoying the vistas reflected in the early afternoon sunlight. The air was fresh, clear, and shimmered against the blue background. Despite the oddity of our meeting I didn't feel any unease or discomfort about sharing an intimate lunch with a person whom was a complete stranger to me. It was Monroe who broke the silence first.

'So what is it exactly that you are looking for? What answers did you expect to find by coming here?' The tone of the question was soft yet firmly directed at me. For several long drawn-out seconds I wasn't sure how to answer.

'My own search is for my inner development; and from this to perceive the truth of life and our reality' I finally said. Monroe nodded with a turn of his mouth, seeming to accept my statement. I was not expecting any response from him; I only felt required to answer in an honest way. Monroe stood up and walked to the edge of the patio, his glass of water in hand. I noticed for the first time how smartly dressed he was. I saw first his shoes; a pair of very fine light brown leather which were clean as a whistle. His white trousers and shirt were without wrinkle, his short white hair pushed back from his face so that I could see what was perhaps the only feature that stood out from him was a sharp nose, almost eagle-like.

'It's a fine thing is truth' Monroe finally said, sipping his water slowly.

'If it can ever be found!' I said, trying to give a chuckle as if I thought my response was ironic. Without pausing Monroe turned to look at me and replied 'Truth is truth; but your reality is what you make it.' The way Monroe said this last statement was so emphatic as if it had been shot at me like an arrow. For some unknown reason it felt as if I had an emotional reaction to what had just been said, for I remember clearly a lump swell in the middle of my chest. I say a lump yet it was not anything physical; rather a ball of heavy energy form momentarily, pulsate several times, then pass away. I looked over at Monroe and he motioned me with his eyes to join him. I stood and walked over to where he was gazing out from the edge of the patio. With his glass in hand he made a brief gesture; 'this is your reality. Everything you see here is for you. This is what you have made – take a look at it.' Yet there was something very odd in the way he spoke, as if his voice was slowed down a fraction so it sounded more blurry. There was a different tone, or resonance, to his voice in this moment. For an instant I wasn't sure where my senses were focused, whether I was straining to hear him or looking out over the vista before me. I was looking down at the garden below that sloped down from the patio. Yet there was something immediately odd about the scene. Then I realized that there was no sound. All was completely silent; almost eerie. I focused my sight onto the garden plants and flowers and I saw then that there was a bird on one of the shrubs. Yet it was still, unmoving. It was then that I sensed everything in my vision was still – silent and still, as if time and motion had frozen. I turned my head to look at Monroe. I think I was wondering whether he too was frozen. But then he turned his head to look at me, and dashed me a quick grin. I turned to look at the garden again and my ears filled with sound and there was a buzz of energy, of life, that had been absent a moment before. Even though the sounds were minimal – the light flow of breeze; a few soft bird calls – they filled my ears in stereo almost as if a once deaf person were switched on to hearing suddenly. I felt relieved at sensing the return of the sounds and energies of life.

'Even such a small tweak of one's sense of reality can be unnerving' continued Monroe once we had sat down again at the table. 'If an unprepared person were to have a full exposure it would literally blow their minds. Such exposure comes with understanding, and a person must be prepared, gradually. It is like waking-up from a deep slumber; like your astronauts from some imagined deep-space hibernation. It can be disorientating – and it can make you crazy!' Monroe looked at me from across the table and raised his eyebrows as if pitying what he was going to say next. 'The truth can make people crazy. That's the way it has always been.' Monroe poured some more water into my now empty glass. 'Truth for many people is what they happen to be thinking in the moment. They have no mechanisms in place for perceiving beyond their limited conditioning. It is difficult to discuss things of which people have no perception of; and thus neither the experience nor the language to frame it. It is like trying to describe the taste of an apple to someone who's never encountered one!' Smiling, he said, 'Tell me, what does *apple* taste like?' I thought for a moment; then knew he had me.

'I see your point. I can't describe the taste. It's kind of juicy, but the apple taste is apple.'

'And you say you would like to find the truth,' continued Monroe, 'when you have yet no capacity to taste the truth. You have expectations, which are no doubt formed from many years of cultural conditioning, mixed with emotions, greed, a dash of need for attention; and topped off by faulty reasoning!' Monroe raised his glass of water and mock-toasted me. I returned the toast.

'Well,' I said, 'seems like the prognosis isn't too bad then after all.' Monroe chuckled, then immediately changed the subject and began talking about the weather in Andalusia. I felt it was a distraction strategy, to take my mind off the current subject, and to allow me to finish eating my lunch in peace, which I did.

It was mid-afternoon as we strolled together to the front gate of the house. The sun was still shining, the light was bright and uplifting, yet the heat was beginning to drain from the day.

'Thank you for the visit' said Monroe as we both stood on the sloping road outside the house. Looking downhill I saw the way we had both walked a couple of hours earlier.

'It was a pleasure. Thank you for the invitation' I replied.

'Oh, how very automatically polite of you!' said Monroe with a smile. 'Your conditioning is quite well formed. Anyway, I wouldn't exactly say that I invited you.' He looked at me blankly.

'What would you say then?' I asked.

'I would say that you brought yourself to my door.'

'Really?' I replied, somewhat surprised by this latest remark. 'So, it's my fault then?'

'Of course not', said Monroe. He was smiling in such a friendly way it was hard not to feel anything but kinship for this man. 'Fault implies a negative trait, and creates guilt within a person. You brought yourself here because it was the right time and right place – only you didn't know it. Anyway, I'm here for a short while so we have time to continue these chats. Next week, same time, come for lunch. Only don't forget to bring your digital recorder with you.' Monroe nodded and began to walk back toward the house. I didn't know what to say. Was it a joke, a bluff? Yet he had said it so confidently, as if it had already been decided.

I began to walk back to the car, trying as hard as I could to remember the details of all that had occurred, and the conversation that had passed between us. It was only when I arrived home I realized I had forgotten to buy a jar of Benamahoma honey.

MEETING TWO

It is true to say I had mixed feelings during the week. I was intrigued with the encounter I had had with the man I now knew as Monroe. And to be fair I also very much enjoyed his company and listening to him. What he said appealed to me. It appealed to my sense of mystery as well as my urge to truly *know* more. I tried to recollect as much of our conversation as possible. What I did manage to remember I wrote down as accurately as I could, despite having the nagging feeling that there were parts I simply could not recall. Hence it was a good idea to bring a recorder for the next meeting.

It was inevitable I would return. I was hooked by the very thing I was greedy for – more information and knowledge. I suspect that Monroe knew this, as he teased me with it; he dangled the bait before me and like a hungry fish I bit the line.

Walking up to the front door I heard Monroe call out, 'Come round the back.' I walked around the house and saw, as I had the week before, a table already immaculately prepared with various dishes of local food to eat. A jug of crystal clear water was standing on the table. Our two chairs and places were set and waiting. Since I knew Monroe to be British and not Spanish I thought it best to greet him formally, so I rigidly stuck out my hand for him to shake.

'How very English of you' remarked Monroe chirpily as he shook my hand. 'So well programmed.' I recognized by now that there was a mocking side to Monroe; a tendency to try to force a reaction through deliberate teases. I was determined to keep my stature and not to play any games, or to play *into* any game.

'And very English of you too to shake my hand' I responded politely with a smile.

'Oh, I'm not English my dear deluded fellow. You are quite wrong, by a wide margin.' I took out my small digital voice recorder, set it to record, and placed it on the table between us. Monroe rubbed his hands in what I took to be a sign of quite youthful delight.

'Well, I congratulate you then as your English is impeccable' I said. This was to be remembered – recorded – as my first opening line for our digital records.

'And I congratulate you too for congratulating me. Isn't this social politeness such a wonderful thing!' said Monroe, smiling at me and raising one of his eyebrows in a gesture that I soon very quickly became accustomed to over our time together.

'Yes, I suppose it is. And so may I ask what is your nationality?'

'Yes, you may ask' replied Monroe as he placed a little food upon his plate. In the silence that followed I observed how he looked exactly as I remembered him from the previous week. His manners were refined and his composure very deliberate; no movement seemed either out of place or an unconscious act. It was as if he was using his body in a precise way, as a hand fits a glove and animates it.

'Okay then – what is your nationality?' I finally asked when it dawned on me the laziness of my language and what the silence had been for.

'I have none' replied Monroe immediately, and took a bite of his bread.

'So then where do you come from; where were you born?' I asked next. Monroe just shook his head.

'You will never get the right answers if you don't learn how to ask the questions you need. You are distracted by irrelevancies and the trivialities of shallow thinking. You need to shift perspective.'

'Okay then,' I said, 'then tell me why you are here.' I watched as Monroe pursed his lips and swayed his head a little from side to side.

'Not bad – although technically not a question. Yet for the sake of details I will take it as a direct question. I am here because I observe the great unfolding that is called life. That does not necessarily imply that I am a nature lover, although I do happen to be. Rather, that my role is to watch how life on this planet is working through its evolutionary journey. I observe the ebb and flow of these processes; where it goes awry; where it needs assistance; and, from time to time, to bring awareness of the nature of this reality to some receptive minds. Now that, in a nutshell as some of you would say, is the *why* I am here.'

'Mmmm' was my muffled response. I nodded my head sagely but actually rather dumbly.

'And if you wanted to know the 'why' I am here in Andalusia, then that is not up for grabs because that is specifics and I am discussing more the bigger picture here. What you need to learn is perspective; especially the perspective of perception of the bigger picture and the nature of your reality – not my specifics which don't concern you.'

'Of course,' I said automatically. I wasn't quite sure what I was after – generality or specifics! In fact, at that moment I remember feeling that I had no idea what it was I either had to ask or should ask.

After all, it was he who had coaxed the repeated meeting into being. Somewhere along the way it was I who was being taken along for the ride. Suddenly my sense of being in control of events evaporated. I realized then that I had been cleverly maneuvered into this situation, and that I had no power or influence to direct the flow of events. It was Monroe who was in charge of this moment; and, I sensed, of all the moments we were to spend together.

'Many people consider it the peak of human development to be kind, generous, to heal the sick and protect the weak' said Monroe as he leaned back in his chair. 'Yet these traits are not spiritual goals but are the elementary social duties incumbent upon humanity as a social animal. Funny how such basic services get lauded and applauded as acts of sainthood. The delinquency of your species is often dressed by the most socially-acceptable behaviour.' Monroe paused before finally adding, 'just an observation mind you. How do you find the food?'

'Mmm...muy bueno' I said as I had a piece of goat's cheese with honey in my mouth. It was artful of how Monroe could make me feel both appreciative and gluttonous in the same moment. A look of embarrassment must have flashed across my face as Monroe made his nodding and chuckling gesture that told me he was both amused and somehow validated by my behaviour.

'One of the issues with humanity, in general, is that it spends so much of its energy and attention trying to tell or persuade each other what to do that individual members are not shown how to find out what particular things need doing to whom, when, and where. A human being has thus put out of its mind the long-term possibility of attaining an objective knowledge of what is happening to humanity. One is inclined to refer to the situation here as being a topsy-turvy world' said Monroe as his eyes moved away to stare at some distant object.

'Yes, it seems that we are back-to-front or upside-down' I began, hoping to get myself involved as a serious participant in this discussion. 'We've come this far, almost to the cusp of a planetary society, globally connected like never before in known recorded history; and now we are on the tipping point of possible collapse. As a global species we are heading for overshoot, meaning going beyond our carrying capacity as a planet.' I had been giving my usual sociological spiel; the same stuff I had been saying over and over again for quite some time.

'Yes, I'm perfectly aware of what overshoot is and how it affects this planet. It is a common feature within the development of civilizations and empires. However, take note that your species did not come this far for nothing. Neither is your species here for your own enjoyment – it has an important function as part of the reciprocity involved in all living systems.' Monroe paused to take a sip of his water in what was a very considerate movement. I stayed silent, chewing quietly, showing no signs of wanting to speak. After a few moments Monroe raised his finger and appeared to point; instinctively I turned my head to gaze in the direction indicated. I saw only the general vista beyond and nothing specific to catch my eye. When I turned back Monroe was shaking his head and smiling to himself. I knew I had been distracted easily.

'The Earth needs a residing species to form a group soul,' continued Monroe. 'That is, for there to be bonds of mutual love, respect, and wisdom between all members of the conscious species so that they act as a unity, whilst also retaining their individual freedom. This is a great cosmic task, and humankind today on your planet represents an early stage in this great undertaking. Now that's not a cue to start thinking in terms of events being orchestrated by some ultimate Godhead, a grand figure that you have humanized by your limited imaginations, sitting upon a throne on high! Your species are only creating role-playing characters by these simplistic thoughts. Neither think in terms of perfection, as such grand evolutionary plans have their flawed moments too. Yet it is safe to say that humankind is nowhere near the capacity able to comprehend what perfection or imperfection means at this level. Your value reasoning is admirable at times, yet terribly burdensome too. It gets in the way of much more balanced comprehension; yet for now you need to keep your sense of duality and polarity, if only as a platform to step beyond these divisive categories.'

'Monroe,' I finally said after a prolonged pause. 'I'm not sure I'm following all of this. Are you saying that you are not human, or at least not from this planet, and that there is a grand evolutionary project going on?'

'You already know everything. Each one of you does; only that it is buried within and access to this knowledge is closed to the majority of your species. The whys of this we will come to. Although you deliberately put a note of surprise in the tone of your question regarding my origin, the fact is that you are not surprised; you felt this to be the case already. So I shall not dwell on this further at this particular moment. Once you come to understand more about how reality functions you will comprehend matters that for now are just slightly beyond your grasp. You have a voice recorder because the amount of information you are receiving is too much to assimilate in one go. Your consciousness will thus store the information and replay it back to you when either the context or the need demands it. Although your brain has a far higher capacity for recording and storage than does this digital device, for the short term you need immediate memory recall of our talks. So don't worry whether you comprehend everything which you will hear from me. It is important you enjoy the ambience of these occasions. The rest will take care of itself. Now,' said Monroe as he rose from his seat, 'did you ever take history classes?'

'Not really,' I replied, 'just a few when I was at school.' I stood up as Monroe walked past and, picking up the voice recorder, followed him as he crossed the patio steps that led onto the lawn below. When we were both on the lawn Monroe turned around and pointed back at the steps.

'You see there how grass and weed is growing through the concrete between the stones?' Monroe asked.

'Yes,' I replied, seeing how there was indeed grass growing through the stone steps.

'Do you know why a living thing grows in the most inhospitable place?'

'No' I said.

'Because it can,' replied Monroe. 'Life is incredible once it is let loose. Now let us put this into perspective and move across the grand picture.' He walked over to a bench that was beneath a hanging tree in the corner of the garden, which I had not previously noted, and sat down. Looking at Monroe sitting there, his legs neatly crossed, I realized for the first time that he was wearing a white Panama hat. Had he been wearing that hat when we met; or during our earlier conversation at the table? For the life of me I couldn't recollect. Not wanting to show my confusion or to question Monroe on the matter I pretended as if I had not noticed the Panama and went to sit down on the bench beside him. Monroe began talking the moment my body touched the bench.

'The history of the Earth shows a slow yet accelerating transformation from lifelessness to life, from primitive sense-forms to developed consciousness. It has not, mind you, always been a smooth journey. There have been profound moments of collapse; yet the adaptation of life on this planet and its ability to immerse itself into its energetic environment is a marvel. You are not the result of mechanical forces, operating blindly within a sea of chance. This is such a disenchanting and, may I say it, post-primitive stage of thinking. I say post-primitive because even the primitive stage is more accepting of the place of life within a grander sacred order. Yet the ignorance that comes later, posing as scientific rationality, is so awkward and dry. It has no scope for the magnificence of love and compassionate wisdom. So you burn your feet trying to reach for the stars through rocket fuel. Amazingly odd!' Monroe cocked his head with a little smile in my direction. 'I guess we're still learning' I said smiling back at him.

'I guess so' said Monroe in a sort of conspiratorial tone. 'Yet,' he continued, 'Life must become responsible for itself. Until that time it must accept the possibility that there are guiding and nurturing forces. Do you really think conscious life made it this far upon its own good fortune? Or perhaps, like many others upon this planet, you believe that it is the survival of the fittest that has been the evolutionary driver, battling away through generations to be top of the evolutionary tree? Really, it's a bit silly, don't you think?'

'Well, I do agree that Darwinism has now been pretty much taken apart by modern science and only a minority now accept a strict Darwinian interpretation' I replied.

'Pretty much. Although more people than you think still adhere to a fundamental Darwinian interpretation of evolution. Creationism or fundamental Darwinism – it's the same mechanisms of extreme beliefs in operation, and the same inflexibility to incorporate new ideas into one's conditioned belief structures. Really, is it so strange to think that there might be an intelligence behind evolution? Many of your scientists often talk of nature as if she is imbued with intelligence; and many of the braver ones actually talk in terms of conscious intelligent fields in nature. So, your fields of thought are gradually getting there. You just need more time for the seeds to develop within your culture. The seeds have already been sown. After all, it is the duty of a nurturing intelligence to make sure that the seeds *are* sown – at the right time and in the right place.'

Monroe slightly raised a finger from his folded hands on his lap as if to emphasize his next remark. 'Growing times, mind you, vary from years to centuries; and sometimes beyond. Farsight is quite amazing when you see it in operation.'

'I have no way to comprehend this' I said after a short pause; 'yet it feels reasonable to me.'

'Reasonable it is' agreed Monroe. 'There are in fact many indicators of this operative design in your own recorded stories. Again, through your polarity lens, you name them as history or myths. History has been used, and abused, to record the past and can be used to connect with a future; whereas myth belongs to the eternal present. Both these carriers of information, streams of code, have woven themselves through your species history as veins supplying your lifeblood. Myths, especially, are part of your genetic inheritance as a species. Thousands of years can pass, your greatest monuments reduced to dust, and yet myths live on as long as there are people in the world. Whatever passes in our conversation as unreasonable for your thinking patterns or unrealistic for your senses, then just put it down as being another myth - a mythology being woven between friends!' Monroe turned to me and gave what I remembered to be such a warm and genuinely affectionate smile. I remember the glow of energy I felt when receiving this smile. And for that brief moment I felt a strong kinship with Monroe that I could not put into words. It was as if I had known this man for such a long time, instead of the few short hours of our meeting.

'At this stage it doesn't really matter whether you *believe* it or not,' continued Monroe, 'as belief is only a category for storing information which you have no rational explanation or science for. It's a convenient little box to place opinions and events that take your fancy, interest you, or are curious about, and yet which you have no credible means to validate. It's amazing how society accepts beliefs, or the right to hold beliefs, no matter how crazy they are, yet has little or no capacity for validating experiential reality. Artificial reality seems to be the general agreed upon true 'one god reality', because it can be uniformly attested to, manipulated, and controlled. Yet the reality that lies beyond the filtering mechanisms of human sense organs – what you call subjective non-ordinary states – are seen as oddities, party talk, or madness. Anyway, you have your myths, and be thankful that these eternal seeds of wisdom remain firmly planted in your species soil. Are you comfortable?' This question coming from out the blue startled me out of my thoughts.

'Yes, thanks, all is good' I replied.

'I didn't ask you if you were good, although I'm glad to hear that too. I asked you if you were comfortable' said Monroe in a detached, non-critical tone. Again, I realized that I had to watch my language when speaking around Monroe as he seemed to treat language as a precise instrument.

'Thank you; yes, I am comfortable' I said.

'Good. Now have you ever considered a form of higher intelligence that enters into humanity?'

'You mean like a kind of possession of human souls?'

'Dear no,' replied Monroe, 'that sounds too much like some religious fear rhetoric; possessing your soul, like those scary feature films you people love to watch. I'm talking of an intelligence that enters into individual or collective minds; you might call it inspiration. Have you never wondered where your thoughts come from? Do you think that all your thoughts are the result of neurons firing inside your head; just some sparks of electric passing through your neuronal passageways? How does humanity account for great leaps of inspiration? Why are there geniuses when everybody is gifted with the same structured brain? Have these such thoughts ever *entered into* your head?'

'Sometimes, yes' I admitted. 'I have often wondered where thoughts originate from and whether they are formed inside the head or can be picked-up from outside.'

'I see' nodded Monroe. 'You tell me that both *sometimes* you think of these things, and also that you have *often* wondered on these matters. Mmm...both sometimes and often. How should I interpret that?' said Monroe as if speaking to himself. Then he turned to me with a big grin, as though letting me know that all was okay. 'Now, let me offer this perspective. Just as the human body is composed of many parts, of different organs with different functions that operate in their own individual ways; when they come together they form a whole, interactive, communicative body. Likewise, think of a color, any color; the color is the same whether it is represented by a drop or an ocean. The essence of living intelligence is simultaneously a part as well as the whole. There are 'parts' of this whole intelligence that can enter into the human being and communicate through both conscious and unconscious thoughts. This is one form of interaction between higher intelligence and humanity that allows for evolutionary guidance to operate.'

'And the other form?' I asked after there had been a suitable pause.

'The other way is indirectly,' continued Monroe. 'It operates through representatives, or emissaries, that are fully human yet developed enough to have the capacity to perceive direct communication with higher intelligence. Such persons weave through life implementing events here and there, being social and, for the most part, passing unnoticed amongst humankind. You need to realize that the essence of a thing is often not what it appears to be. Thus, there has always by necessity, and design, been those on your planet who can *see* – ironically, though, *you* don't see *them!*'

'Why is that, are they invisible?' I asked innocently. At this remark Monroe chuckled quite audibly.

'No, it's because they are completely normal, and people are usually on the lookout for something that fits their twisted imaginations. Of course, you have plenty of suppliers for this ongoing demand. A word of advice – always watch out for the weird ones! They usually have too much of both beard and egos. Yet we are moving ahead of ourselves. To resume, evolution began slow as Intelligence first entered into the beginnings of life more than two billion years ago.'

'Are you saying that this Intelligence created life on the planet?' I asked. Monroe turned his head slightly to look at me.

'Ohh, isn't that such a crazy thought!', he whispered. 'Imagine intelligence creating life; well, we can't have that, can we? Surely it is more plausible to think that life was created from non-life? A non-living accidental process just happens to create the spark of life that over billions of years creates semi-intelligent apes. I think this must be the only possible explanation to account for the dimness of the human race. What do you think?'

'I think you must be right' I whispered back. I had hoped I was correct in catching his irony. I had the strong feeling that Monroe was always several steps ahead.

'Your scientists are fond of dallying in the laboratory, trying to prove one thought-form after another. Yet in many cases they fail to observe the one consistent proof – that results are generally obtained by intervention from above. That is, not from some divine intervention but from the scientists hovering above the experiment. Does not your own understanding of quantum physics tell you that observers alter the experiment? There can be no vacuum in such matters; the role of the scientists is more crucial than you think, although in ways that you perhaps do not imagine. That they observe their objects actually makes their results subjective and not objective as they have always claimed. You cannot take out the presence of consciousness. Another point is that life, as you know of it, is directed toward a goal. It does not exist purely for its own sake; or worse, for nothing. Why are you looking at me strangely? Your expression tells me you think I've gone god-soppy.'

'I didn't think I was looking at you in any particular way', I replied defensively.

'I was not referring to an expression on your face. I don't need to see a pattern of wrinkles to know how a person is looking. The way you were looking at me with your thoughts. You were jumping into the perception-set of conditioned religious definitions. Do you think I am telling you that all life follows a Divine purpose? Why are you internally processing what I say through religious filters?' Monroe was now looking at me directly, his face unmoving and without expression. I had no idea what to make of the moment, or what he was expecting from me. I managed to collect my thoughts and say 'So life is directed? Then why does evolution have its stops and starts; its extinctions?'

'Good point', said Monroe with a wide, friendly smile. 'And why can't false evolutionary starts be part of a directed process? Again, this goes back to your conditioning that such 'higher Intelligence' should be perfect, etc, etc, blah, blah. As I've said, we're not talking of an ultimate Intelligence here...but an Intelligence-guided process. Of course there will be failed attempts. Evolution is itself a learning curve, wouldn't you say?'

'In that sense, yes I would. So it can be said that evolution is about an Intelligence pervading life forms on this planet?' I was trying now to watch my words carefully. I could see, or more to the point sense, that Monroe was observing very closely our interaction and my manner of addressing this subject.

'In a basic sense, yes.' Monroe began to chuckle to himself; and turning his head to face me wagged his gaunt finger in my direction – 'which means that all of you are also alien to some degree. No escaping it now – the alien cat is out the bag!' Monroe laughed and took in a deep breath and appeared to take great delight in the surrounding nature. For what appeared to be a prolonged moment

Monroe gazed into the leaves of the tree hanging above him. In this silence I noticed for the first time, since our time in the garden earlier, the sounds of the birds. There was a chorus of tweeting, of bird calls, of great activity. My brief reverie was broken by Monroe's voice.

'If life was solely about the birth, life, and death of animal bodies, nothing animating them but blood and survival instincts, then life on this planet could be called 'native'. It would also be operating for quite another purpose. In your terms you would perhaps refer to it as "meaningless". It is somewhat ironic that your species is now in the fuzzy zone.'

'The fuzzy zone! What's that exactly?' I asked generally surprised.

'Well, you are occupying a "fuzzy space" between both worlds. In your, let us call it, pre-historic times your ancestors had a highly developed instinctual sense. The early Neanderthal breed was in fact a moon-worshipping matriarchal society, sensitive to the moon's influence upon the Earth. The Cro-Magnon breed that came later, and which sought to eliminate the Neanderthals, were sun-worshippers and patriarchal. Although both deemed highly primitive by your standards they had keener instincts in terms of sensing life as intractably bound with external solar and cosmic forces. Whereas the 40,000 years Homo Sapiens Sapiens breed has developed the civilization model, taken progress by the horns and run with technological ingenuity; yet remains instinctually stunted. Interesting that such a pinnacle of physical evolution should display arrested development in the psychic faculty. Anyway, to continue, the process of evolution is an experiment of the manifestation of Intelligence within matter. This manifestation can be most clearly seen by following the evolution of human consciousness.'

'So does that mean that evolution on this planet is more or less the evolution of consciousness?' I asked Monroe.

'More or less? That's quite a useful abstract phrase – it's the type of phrase one uses, I imagine, when one is fishing for answers yet has nothing on the end of their line. More or less is also useful in presenting concepts that are too obtuse for the listener to comprehend, thereby softening the edges. So, yes, more or less – let us say – evolution of material forms on this planet goes hand in hand with the process of emerging consciousness. The manifestation of Intelligence within material forms brings a unity of spirit through a diversity of form. The current physical model for this manifestation of unity consciousness on this planet is humankind. If this process is successful, which, by the way, is the plan, then Earth humankind will have evolved into a new soul-species – another unitary Intelligence. It is quite remarkable that at this stage in the process the majority of humankind is still oblivious to any notion of spirit, or of inter-dimensional life and intelligence.

Your many prophets and mystics have been right in saying that you are living in a state of collective amnesia. It is a deep sleep, this sense of isolated physical existence, and you must awaken from it. A species of sleepwalkers imagining nothing exists beyond the boundaries of their tiny blue planet, and nothing beyond their limited five senses. Why do you create this illusion? Did a mental disease strike your planet?'

I had to laugh. 'Yes', I said, 'We've all been put under a collective hypnotic trance!'

'You may indeed laugh', continued Monroe, 'yet this is closer to the truth, literally, than you know. There are forces which are not too happy about what is transpiring on this planet, and where Intelligence is going. There are forces attempting to forestall this program. Anyway, no more on this matter now. I wouldn't wish to alarm your imaginative minds and send you off onto flights of fancy...more or less.'

'But isn't it good to have imaginative minds, to be creative in thought? Why shouldn't we stimulate this?' I replied, not wanting Monroe to leave the subject too soon.

'Indeed, creativity is one of the higher facets of consciousness. It was the access to creativity that marked out a higher stage of development in species evolution. The ability to manifest the interior realm onto the world outside is a huge step in evolution.

Your ancestral cave paintings are examples of this early emergence of creativity. It is a form of translating what lies beyond the senses into a form communicable within the physical. You guys are still doing it today, with various levels of success I might add!' After saying this Monroe stood up and made an exaggerated motion of stretching his arms wide as if he had just stepped out of a cramped cocoon. Then shaking his legs in a somewhat playful style he began to stroll away from the bench. I got up and fell in beside him. Monroe then made for a tour of his flower garden, smelling the petals and checking, or caressing, the stalks. He appeared to be observing the flowers in great detail. I almost did not wish to disturb him, as if it was a ritual he was engaged in. Yet I knew I had to keep the line of conversation alive, and progressing. All of it was leading somewhere, I was sure.

'You mentioned about the early cave paintings. Was that the early signs of creative consciousness?' I asked. Monroe continued to check his flowers a moment longer, and did not lift up his head when he spoke.

'In your terms yes, it was. However, such cave drawings were not the scribbles of any passer-by who happened to be taken by a brief moment of inspiration. There is a cave, and then there is a cave – not every cave is the same. What I mean by this is that your human collective imagination, what you also ironically refer to as your history, has this image of all 'primitive' ancestors living in family caves – a type of Fred Flintstone caricature. In fact caves were sacred places – they were sacrosanct to many, and can be regarded as early forms of temples. Only the initiated were allowed to penetrate to the heart of such caves where you see the remarkable drawings. I'm not talking about minor scribbles on cave entrances; I'm talking here of the profound insights found in such caves as at Lascaux and Chauvet in France. These works of the imaginal mind are around 32-35,000 years old.'

'Wow', I gasped, 'I never realized such paintings were that old! So, these were the creative drawings from the conscious mind of the early, eh, priests?'

'Yes, they were. Since access to such caves was forbidden except to the initiated, they were the forerunners to later priestly elites. Yet I think a better word to use is custodians of a tradition, as they were guardians of consciousness rather than some religious script. Let me give you an example in deciphering their images. In Lascaux there is a depiction of deer crossing a river. Whereas orthodox interpretation believes it shows how your ancestors were mirroring their hunting lifestyle, it actually is a depiction of an initiation rite – crossing a river that separates one realm from the other. Also, if your kind cared to look more closely, you would notice that the deer had antlers: the number of antlers on each deer would correspond to the level of development of the person whose emblem they were. This deep symbolism is a language that sought to manifest the realm of Intelligence with the domain of matter. These early custodians – you may also call them shamans - held great power amongst the tribes as their knowledge helped to maintain cohesion within what was a harsh and cruel environment. Yet that was a time long ago...before the ice started to melt.'

'When was this?' I asked quickly. My curiosity was being drawn in as a hungry man to food. Monroe straightened himself up and narrowed his eyes at me. 'Intelligence before wisdom' he muttered quietly under his breath. I didn't know exactly what he was referring to. When he noticed by blank expression he began to smile and patted me fatherly on the shoulder.

'Well, the great glaciers across the Earth slowly melted over many thousands of years. This was a harsh time for hominid life on this planet. At this time there occurred what we can refer to as a Withdrawal. From the end of the last Ice Age - 10,500 BCE to around 8,000 BCE - there was a withdrawal of evolutionary Intelligence and a concentration, or rather storage of it, waiting for a more opportune time for its dispersal amongst humankind.'

'That sounds odd', I ventured to say. 'I've never heard of such a concept before.'

'It may sound odd to you', replied Monroe, 'because you are not versed to such operations. Yet it should not be unfamiliar to you. A very similar withdrawal occurred in more recent times, during what became termed by historians as the Dark Ages in Europe. When external conditions are not ripe, then energy and knowledge is withdrawn from general circulation and concentrated in specific 'centers', until such time when it can be suitably released according to geographical variations. I know you look puzzled. Don't think on it too much now; it is only superfluous information for you. You can't process it or do anything with it right now, so just shelve it in your mind for when it will be needed.'

'Sure, fine. I can't really grasp the concept anyway; so maybe it's not for me to understand right now. Anyway, what happened after the last Ice Age?'

'Well, your text books can tell you all this. After the retreat of the ice, which opened up more fertile land, the new phase of global warming that occurred created a geographical area better suited for a new climate of growth. Especially fertile land – hence called the Fertile Crescent – was around the Tigris, Euphrates, and Jordan valleys in what is now southwest Asia. Soon you had domesticated plants and animals evolving in these areas which made it easy for people who lived there to become farmers. People in this region were seen by your historians as being the first to settle in villages, prior to 9000 BCE. In a sense, this phase in the cultural evolutionary process instigated the first "modern" wave of social development. Mind you, there were a number of different observation teams on the ground, and elsewhere, noting all this taking place. It is like being in a garden in springtime, watching as the first flowers bloom. There we observed the first patches of growth in the new model of human civilization. It was exciting times. Many of the observation teams had high hopes for this new creative impulse.' Monroe moved away from the flower beds and walked back up the steps to his patio, shaded by overhanging vines. The sun was getting hot now, surprisingly warm for this early spring. I couldn't tell if Monroe enjoyed the heat or not. He appeared to move around under the sun easily enough, and without noticeable discomfort; yet he never stayed too long under its direct gaze. We both sat down once again at the table. Although still littered with the remnants of our lunch, I was hungry now for other and different types of food.

'We were right to have hope', began Monroe after a sip of iced water, 'because by the 4th millennium BCE the first city-states emerged in the river valleys of Egypt and Mesopotamia, with irrigation and innovative husbandry. Did you know that the earliest city-states in Uruk, around 3,500 BCE, and later Sumer and Egypt, displayed some of the earliest known records of energy-intensive urban organization?' I shook my head. I wasn't sure if it was in wonder or disbelief. The statement just seemed to go over my head. So I just raised my eyebrows and nodded my head; sagely or stupidly I couldn't be sure.

'Ah, well, perhaps not. Well, soon your ancestors had their networks of cities spread through what you know now as Syria and the Levant, and through Iran. Fortified towns began springing up along the south-eastern coast of here, Spain. Then within what seemed like a blink of an eye, around the 2nd millennium BCE, long-distance trade sprang up and exploited the Mediterranean's waterways and expanded west. Expansion, and more expansion – that's the way it has always gone. This pattern can be easily maintained when you are dealing with regional manifestations; more difficult when you come to the planetary stage. But that's for later. When you step back you can see the now familiar pattern that human civilization passes through: more local resources create larger populations; this leads to more complex lifestyles and the increased need for resources; military power is needed to gain and secure more extensive resources; which inevitably leads to colonization and empire building. So your modern world's great civilizations all go back to these original episodes of domestication at the end of the last Ice Age.'

'Is human civilization such an obvious pattern? Are we that easy to define? I mean, it's almost as if you can see us coming!' I gestured with a forced half-laugh. Monroe just smiled back.

'More or less. Of course, there are those whom, in your words, 'see you coming'; yet that is not surprising when they have been involved in guiding you to come. Patterns are important in that from seeing only a small part of a pattern it is possible to discern the bigger picture. It is similar to your science of fractals whereby a small segment of the part contains the whole design.'

'And like the hologram too? That's the same in that a small piece of the hologram contains the image of the whole' I said.

'Exactly. The hologram is a precise tool for understanding the patterns within your reality as it represents the underlying field of connectivity from which your materiality manifests…anyway, a pleasant distraction; although not one we shall immediately concern ourselves with now. Are you sure you are quite full from lunch – would you wish for anything more?'

'Oh, no, that's fine thanks. I'm good' I replied.

'You are good? How good are you? Do you mean that the devil won't be dragging you away!' laughed Monroe. I smiled, knowing that Monroe was yet again teasing me for my lazy use of words.

'Thank you', I said in a deliberate manner. 'I have eaten well and I am full.'

'Good' said Monroe, a large smile erupting across his face. 'Let me tell you that your species is quite remarkable. Homo sapiens sapiens have imposed their will on the environment in ways beyond all other creatures on the Earth. You have adapted quickly to the pattern of capturing and organizing your energy resources; then forming villages; expanding into cities, states, and finally empires across the planet. It is like a software program that multiples itself exponentially.' Monroe gives me a quizzical look here before continuing. 'To think that from the various evolutionary attempts to develop a species capable of manifesting creative consciousness, we arrive at a global species that is apparently so different externally, with alternative colors, sizes, adjustments, and yet the genetic differences between modern humans in different parts of the world is negligible. Oh, I know you play your games of differences, and you spread your awful rumors and strange beliefs about superiority, and ancestry and all that – yet none of you are fundamentally different from the other. And this is important, vitally so. It is important because the genetic physical expression shares a fundamental design which enables a group soul to form. You are a species nuclear family...' Monroe paused a moment. 'We really do hope that one day this realization will make you behave toward yourselves better.'

'I hope so too', I agreed. 'You would think so after such a long journey. I can only guess that we didn't come this far for nothing.'

'You are right on that point. You did not evolve to this stage for nothing. Of course, it was never guaranteed that you would evolve to this stage at all! Several of the earlier attempts…well, let us say they petered out. Yet it is difficult to foresee exact environmental conditions and circumstances. There were periods where conditions on this planet were conducive, and where earlier tribes lived in peace and in a stable relationship to nature. As I have said, your Neanderthal ancestors, despite the brutish depiction by your archaeological savants, were really a decent breed.'

'I wouldn't call them our ancestors', I said hastily. 'They were wiped out and replaced by the Cro-Magnon – didn't you say that earlier?'

'I did indeed allude to this, in a general way. What I did not say though, and I will say it now, is that part of the Neanderthal strain was absorbed into the Cro-Magnon stock by sexual interbreeding.'

'Really? I've never heard of that.'

'You may not have heard of it because it is not accepted as your general knowledge. However, it does not negate the truth of a fact. It happened to be the case that the Cro-Magnon men found the highly-sexed Neanderthal females excellent mating partners. So if you have the DNA of homo sapiens sapiens checked for traces of Neanderthal DNA you will certainly find it there. There are some things that cannot be hidden. So you have come this far, and it took a lot of earlier attempts to find a species body most suitable. And you have been blessed by this window of opportunity. Since the end of the last Ice Age your environmental conditions have been, to use one of your own words, lush. These few thousand years have seen incredible development, and it has been within such a speck of evolutionary time. This is the rising crest of consciousness on this planet, which is why it is of such great interest to so many others. For hundreds of thousands of years there was so little development in the way of creativity, or the means for Intelligence to manifest through physicality here. Yet this changed about 40,000 years ago – with you!' said Monroe spreading his hands open in my direction. Again, I had nothing to say to this except another sage/stupid nod of my head.

'And so we have this pattern of expansion and civilization that has gone through a few mini-cycles of explosion and implosion. And then boom! You have the Industrial Revolution that triggered such a rapid phase; quite remarkable, and thoroughly interesting for all to observe. The last 12,000 years or so the human species has been living in an intervening era between the last Ice Age and what could potentially be a stage of collective planetary soul. You could say that the last 12,000 years have been an evolutionary program that has taken humanity from early foragers into forging an evolutionary conscious unity. It really has been the most rapid rise imaginable, with the last two centuries being an incredible accelerating burst. And then you end the 2nd millennium CE, as you name it, with two of the most spectacular shows of arrogance and brilliance: the atomic bomb and spaceflight. Now, that really piqued our interest and we just had to come en masse.'

'Which got your interest?' I asked unsure; 'the atomic bomb or our spaceflight?

'Both actually' answered Monroe. 'In some ways they are equally dangerous for you, and for us...'

Monroe paused, and then stood and walked to the edge of the patio. I was intrigued for him to carry on this line of the conversation. Somehow he seemed to sense that now it was I who was piqued; yet he appeared to drop all talk of the subject. He beckoned me toward him, and then walked me onto the small path away from the patio and around to the front area of the house.

'We have only been talking so far about the physical side of things. This is the small universe. This is the realm of droplets, but is not the ocean. You are surrounded by a vastness you are unable to see. It is time to begin taking off your blinkers. Just like those horse blinders that you crazy folk put on your equestrian friends when racing them for your perverse delight. These artificial constructs prevent your horses from seeing to the rear and, often enough, to the side. Your trainers like to keep the horse focused on what is in front of him, forcing the horse to pay attention to specific stimuli, and thus to stay in the race. The same applies to your species as a whole. Blinkered and blinded you run around peddling your amnesia like it is golden nectar. More sad than amusing I'm afraid. However, it is but a temporary state. And it is time that these limitations were thrown off. There is great change coming.'

By this time I realized that we had reached the front gate of the house. I turned and looked at Monroe, not knowing if this was indeed my cue to leave. Monroe seemed to know my slight hesitation. Putting his hand gently on my shoulder he said, 'Not good to overload. We'll speak more next time. Can you come in three days?'

'Yes, sure' I said. I felt Monroe's grip on my shoulder become firmer, and I felt a wave of friendship enter into me. He turned around and disappeared behind the house once more. I felt gratitude and appreciation for Monroe; and I knew he was being incredibly patient with me. Perhaps he had been incredibly patient with all of us for such a long time.

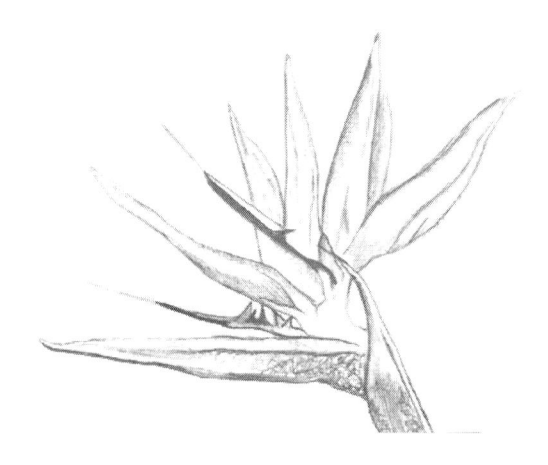

MEETING THREE

THREE days later I was again at the gate of Monroe's white Andalusian house. It was an exceptionally lovely day; bright sunshine and a slight breeze. I had transcribed the notes from our previous meeting, and had been amazed at how much I had forgotten from our actual chat. It appeared that the human mind was indeed coming up short in its ability to retain information. This was something I wanted to bring up with Monroe at our third meeting. So I was eager for yet another lunchtime talk.

As I placed my hand upon the gate to open it I heard Monroe's unmistakable voice call out. 'Be with you shortly. No need to come in!' I paused, and looked around the road where I stood. There was no-one else about. Why was I suddenly feeling so self-conscious, as if worried that others may see me standing here? I tried deliberately to look casual by inspecting the border fence that had lavender and rosemary bushes growing through. I bent down to smell them, immediately remembering Monroe's own actions with his flower bed. A sudden moment of focus entered me then, and my mind noted a blaze of colors, sounds, and scents.

'So much is missed' came Monroe's voice from behind. 'It is filtered out by your brain. Fine shame! Now, let us get moving. We are going on a little walk today' said Monroe as he greeted me with a smile and a now familiar hand upon the shoulder. Fine, I thought, a walk it shall be.

Monroe was dressed in smart yet casual white attire; his short-sleeved shirt revealing healthily tanned arms. On his head he wore his white Panama hat. For the first time I noticed that he had on a pair of darkened sunglasses so that I could not see his eyes. There was nothing about this man – or rather this figure – that would cause anyone to suspect he was anything other than ordinary. His ordinariness, in fact, was his perfect disguise.

'Here, take this' said Monroe as he held a small backpack out to me. I took the pack, which wasn't very heavy, and fell into step beside him as he strolled off up the road. I was grateful for the slight breeze that we had that day. Monroe and I walked together in silence for what must have been the best part of an hour. It was not a strenuous walk; rather a meander through a shaded trail that followed a lower part of the mountain range. There seemed to be no reason to speak. There was no compunction to do so, and I felt comfortable walking with Monroe, observing our surroundings. Physically Monroe was a fit man; and although it was hard to be sure of his age I had the feeling he was older than he looked. And yet I also had to dismiss these thoughts since I couldn't be sure that Monroe was even from the same mould as the rest of us…and such categorizations seemed irrelevant.

  We eventually came across the stone ruins of an old building, perhaps some farmer's barn. There was no roof, only the walls remaining, and Monroe sat down under the shade of one of the walls.

'There are some refreshments in the sack' said Monroe. I sat down near to him and brought out some fruit, dried fruit, bread, cheese, salami, and a flask of chilled water. For this moment, the refreshments were perfect.

'Did you see those eagles hovering high in the sky?' asked Monroe, sipping a flask-head of water.

'Ah, so they were eagles. I wasn't sure, being far away. But I think I saw them' I replied.

'So you think you did?' said Monroe, nodding his head as though pondering my reply. 'And what else did you *think* you saw?' I realized now what Monroe was getting at. Another slip in my laziness of language! However, I didn't wish to take the bait too easily.

'Well, I saw the different flowers; the wild bushes and herbs; some mountain goats up there on the higher ledges; some rabbit shit...

'It was sheep shit' interrupted Monroe, not even looking at me. His gaze was out over the wall and away in some distant place.

'Okay, some sheep shit, and ....' I paused. I had to think now of what else I had seen. I had the feeling then that Monroe wanted to impart something, to tell me something, so I slipped out the digital recorder that had been in my pocket and placed it on the floor between us. I noticed a slight smile from the edge of Monroe's mouth, as if he knew what I had just done; yet he continued to look away.

'People on this planet', began Monroe, 'are living at the moment in a realm of distortion. This means that people have to make use of the resources and capacities they have, in the here and now, to find their sense of direction. There is no immediate way of getting out of this, no escape hatch. It is every person's responsibility to adapt their lives, within this parody of a "life", toward what is a real aim. We each must play our part whilst we are here; like a play the parody must be played out. Yet at the same time, a correct alignment - or orientation - with another form of reality must be made a goal of effort. There has never been any other true objective available to planetary humanity.'

I couldn't quite grasp the entirety of what Monroe had just said. Although only a few words I sensed there was an enormity of information there. Then a big question came to my mind as a response.

'What is the destiny of humankind?' I asked. For the first time since sitting down Monroe turned to look at me.

'It is not possible in your language to give a direct answer to this; nor would I attempt an answer in any verbal manner. You see, the question does not warrant an answer in the medium in which it is asked. If I gave you an answer in order to satisfy your curiosity it would not benefit you internally, because you had not worked yourself to achieve the answer. To be given something without gaining it does disservice to the essence of the thing itself. Further, not only can it not be appreciated in this way, it can not be assimilated neither. An answer to that which you seek can only be arrived at through one's own travel; then the answer will be clothed in the taste of this travel, for the individual to absorb. The truth is the truth, yet there are as many roads to it as there are human hearts. How do you like the fruit, I bought it fresh this morning?'

'Oh yes, lovely' I replied as I was munching on a juicy pear. Then I realized, of course too late, that I had been distracted at the last moment from his answer. For some reason the answer had impacted me, I felt it was profound, and yet I was unable to feel the impact because I had been diverted away at the final moment. I felt robbed of an emotional reaction. I *sensed* an impact from Monroe's answer, yet I had no emotional blow on which to chew on.[1]

'What is primary to realize', continued Monroe with hardly a time for myself to respond, 'is that humankind is operating within a highly limited range of perception. The great proportion of reality is closed-off to you. Like a reducing valve your senses only allow a small sliver of perception to enter. Your reality is thus a tiny part of a much grander picture. It is like looking at a single pixel on a screen and trying to make out the complete form. The reality you operate within is this single pixel; and it limits you terribly. Really, the world is inside your head. You decode the world.'

'I can see that; how the world exists for us. I don't expect that a dog, for example, sees the same world as we...', I paused there; 'or I mean I do.'

'Quite right – perceptive and smart', smiled Monroe as he leaned with his back against the stone wall. 'It really is a beautiful day. And

---

[1] It was only later when I re-played the recording that I could more fully listen and digest what Monroe had said. This was the same for most of our conversations. Yet listening to the conversation digitally, after the moment, had the effect of reducing the emotional impact from the statements. I could not be sure if this was Monroe's deliberate intention or not.

there are parts of this beauty that exist for human senses too; even though there is no standard even between you humans.'

'Surely there must be standards' I objected. 'What about this green grass – wouldn't all humans perceive and agree on this?'

'Not if you were color-blind' replied Monroe. I couldn't see but I sensed a smile.

The mountains in this area were stony, with patches of the slopes covered in swathes of trees. I could imagine the heat bearing down here in the peak of summer. It would be a sweltering heat; the kind that makes you sweat before you begin to move. Yet in the spring breeze it was ideal, and allowed for motionless silence too that was comfortable.

'Are you painting the world?' asked Monroe after a long silence between us.

'I'm just gazing out; wondering how it is that everything I see is but a slim part of the whole' I replied in a somewhat distant voice.

'You and everybody else', said Monroe briskly. 'The world as you know it – *your world* – is painted by you; by billions of painters stocked with a very limited palette of only a few colors. That is why you paint a grim picture' said Monroe grinning.

'And is that entirely our fault?' I asked somewhat defensively. 'I mean, we are at the mercy of our senses; and if we have limited senses we have limited perceptions.'

'I would rather put it that you have limited perceptions because you have limited sense', replied Monroe with a dead-pan expression. 'Let us not get into the fault-game', he continued. 'Let us first acknowledge and agree that human senses at their general state of functionality are only able to perceive a very small portion of the electromagnetic spectrum. This small portion gets filtered through a range of processes – we can call it pattern-recognition – that then provides a picture of reality that conforms to both the senses and one's conditioned set of patterns. These "perceptions" are then analyzed and interpreted by you numskulls through an even finer sieve of conditioned patterns called human thinking. What comes out at the end of this labyrinth of obscurity and psychosis is a picture of reality that's closer to Salvador Dali than anything else.'

'Mmm' I mumbled, nodding my head yet not sure how to respond. 'I guess then that we need to evolve our perceptive functions and patterns of recognition.'

'You surely do. And until that time most of you will sadly be walking around with blinkers on. You see, reality as you call it is not something solid that exists *out there*. You seem to think that the world is an immovable object. The "world" comes into being through perception. The core aspect of reality is that everything is vibrational information. Everything is just waveform. Reality is a sea of energy from which universes ripple on the surface. Do you remember as a kid sitting on the beach and watching a wave roll in from the sea toward the shore?' asked Monroe.

'Sure. It used to be one of the few things I would do if I ever went to a beach. Sit and watch each wave coming in from far off; and crash when it hit the sand.'

'Yet the vision of a wave rolling over the ocean until it finally reaches the shore is an illusion. It is not one wave that comes galloping across the water. The wave does not move; it is the sea, a blanket of water that lifts and falls and gives the impression of a moving wave.' Saying this Monroe took the cloth that had wrapped the fruit and ran his finger beneath it; and I watched as a peak ran across the surface of the cloth. 'What you interpret as a solid object moving above the sea of energy is rather the effect when the bed of energy rises. You perceive objects rather than the underlying energy that connects. And by focusing on the appearance of objects you become sucked into a sense of isolation; of a world that is static and devoid of connective energy. Humankind needs to realize that the world they live in is not static, even though it *may appear* so to them. A person can control very little of their circumstances, and the things which happen to them. However hard a person may strive, the impacts of the environment around them are constantly changing and having an effect on their life. In order to cope better in the world each person should learn to become more flexible and versatile – to bend in the wind like a willow tree, I think is one of your expressions. Also, to not treat transient things as the end and be all of everything; it would be better to treat the transient as the constant in human life. The fleeting is the norm, and yet so many of you cling to totems and objects as if they were the enduring elements of a life. And so your life becomes vulnerable because its stability relies on untrustworthy things. This is why you lot are constantly in fear, whether you recognize this or not. Deep down you know that you cling to the fleeting, and yet to let go seems to bewilder you. It is an odd condition to observe. Frankly speaking, I find myself both amused and bemused by this behaviour.'

'Do we make you sad Monroe?' I asked.

'No' he smiled. 'You just make me crazy.'

Leaving the ruins we continued along the half-worn path as the sun bounced off our faces. Neither of us spoke for a long while. I followed slightly behind Monroe as he weaved a course as sure as a ship's captain. I kept my eyes on him, not knowing if at some sudden moment he would shoot off and leave me there not knowing the path. I wouldn't put this past him, and I chuckled to myself at how devious he could no doubt be. I continued to be surprised at Monroe's agility, and began to forget his appearance as an 'older man'. After some time we came to an old stone bridge that straddled a small river, now almost a stream. Monroe did not cross but stopped at its beginning.

'This is a bridge' said Monroe turning to me. I nodded my head. 'And over there is the Real. And we are here, on the side of the world of appearances. We need to cross the bridge to the Real. The world that you live in acts as this bridge to the Real, yet it is not the Real. Everything you need to cross to the Real exists here in this reality, and can help you if you learn how to use it. Appearances are a bridge to the Real. You must work at polishing this bridge, within and without yourself. Without this polishing, there will be no bridge. You have everything you need. As for now, you have two feet…so let's walk across.' And we did.

Stopping beneath the shade of a large sprawling tree I sat beside Monroe as we gazed down the slope. Not far below us stood a small white town nestled against the hills. It was Benamahoma, the Andalusian town where Monroe lived - and our destination.
'Not far now' said Monroe with a slight nod of the head. I looked closely at his face. It was unblemished; clear of sweat, strain, or stress. The eyes were gazing into the distance, placid yet intense. I

wasn't sure if he was observing some minute feature in the world outside of him; or at some place within, or elsewhere.

'Can a person learn to perceive the Real, as if bit by bit?' I asked.

'Mmm....yes', murmured Monroe quietly. He seemed preoccupied with some other thought. Then suddenly, as if snapping out of some daze, he threw me a quick grin. 'Picture this: you are sitting in an airplane, eating a sandwich. The airplane, you and the sandwich are hurtling through the air at several hundred miles per hour. You are completely unaware of this, of course, unless you happen to look out of the window and see a fixed point below. Yet the human body does not register the velocity through the air as it does not *appear* to affect you. This immersion within the physical dimension of incredible speed is unperceived. This, in a way, shows how the existence of another dimension can operate alongside of you, yet it goes by relatively unnoticed. It is there, its very existence maintains you, it keeps you in the air, yet for various reasons you are not picking it up. Or rather, something within you is choosing not to recognize it. We are immersed in this other dimension all the time, like the air we breathe, and yet most people are completely oblivious to it. Only when a glitch appears and some unexplained phenomenon occurs do we notice something odd suddenly happening in our reality. Yet once this brief rip in the veil is gone our senses go back to sleep again, as if the anomaly were a dream.

All this happens without the least attention from people; it's quite amazing. Now, if you are able to fix your attention and to discern the presence of the anomalies when they occur, they will gain permanence for you. When this permanence of phenomena grows more and more within your current reality field what will happen is that you will be shifting your perceptual state to another dimension of reality. It is there, has always been there; only that your species has been veiled to its operation.'

'Yet some people, as you say, have noticed these anomalies in our current reality field?'

'Yes', replied Monroe; and then chuckled. 'The less astute ones took themselves off to lie on the couches of equally less astute ones; only to make a double mess of things!' I laughed with Monroe at the thought of a psychiatrist trying to convince the patient that their glimpse of Reality had really been a subconscious sexual desire from their early oral stage manifesting!

'Well....we at least have researchers who've been trying to unveil this stuff for ages' I said somewhat abstractly.

'Oh yes, why of course. Your species have such intrepid interpreters by the truck load. You have a library of Congress filled with your incessant interpretations. You have even created an industry of people to bicker over and prance around interpretations of interpretations. You call them scholars!' Monroe said with obvious delight and a broad open grin on his face. He was, it seemed, enjoying this ridicule. I couldn't say I didn't blame him.

'I guess you can't blame them for trying' I replied. As soon as I had said it though, I realized it was a rather blasé, shallow remark. Why had I said it? Monroe turned to look at me; his face expressionless. Slowly he raised his eyebrows in a way that made me feel patronizingly small.

'I guess I can't blame *you*', said Monroe slowly, articulating each word, 'for replying automatically with empty words. It is, after all, what your society trains you to do.'

'Yes, not my best words' I admitted.

'Unless you know that another reality exists; and unless you learn how to seek its existence, you will always tend to pursue the appearance' continued Monroe.

'And is this what religion and spirituality have been doing over the millennia?' I asked

'It is to the degree they had an attraction in their core towards the Real. Yet in most cases this kinetic core either became crystallized or buried under layers of social soot. That which is truly spiritual, and belongs to the realm of real higher consciousness, is difficult to maintain in this physical world. It is for this reason that most of the manifestations of religion and supposed spirituality end up as either caricatures or stripped and turned into social institutions.'

After saying this Monroe handed me the flask of water. 'You are sitting in the shade and yet I see you are sweating.'

'Well, it is a hot day. Nothing mysterious there' I replied jokingly.

'Nothing mysterious at all', agreed Monroe. 'Just a shame you can't have a decent conversation with a bloke these days without them coming out in globules of urea.'

'Is that the main problem we have then?'

'No, not the main one' replied Monroe with his characteristic smile. 'One of the main ones is that humankind has largely forgotten that they have the capability of attaining an objective knowledge of what is happening to them, and their place in the grander scheme of things. Therefore they have come to believe that such a view is not even possible. Humans, in general, are so conditioned that they want to fight against the current structures of reality only to replace them with more structures of the same. They play with old models not understanding that they are dealing with the obsolete. It is a roundabout tale of the status quo bashing against its own four walls. Dumb pleasures!'

'Yet don't you think we are getting there? I mean, where we are today in our thinking is at least an improvement from the past'.

'Yes, of course it is an improvement' replied Monroe with a gentle wave of his hand. 'The question is upon what scale, and according to the value of time. A small improvement over a long period of time is not what one would call a most satisfactory leap forward. You can not always deal with generalities. We need specifics. We need more of the *do be do*, and less of the *blah blah blah*.'

I had to laugh at this. Monroe put on a mocking tone, making the 'blah' sound like an elongated *bluurgh*. Monroe himself began to chuckle, seemingly relaxed. 'You may laugh', he said between his own chuckling, 'yet it is so true. Go almost anywhere today and what do you hear coming out of people's mouths? It is just the same *blah blah blah*, day after day. I wouldn't mind so much but the majority of it is not even amusing. In fact it is fearful!'

'What do you mean by "fearful"? That it makes you afraid of listening to them?' I queried.

'No, rather the opposite - it makes people afraid from listening to their own words. People often talk themselves into fearful thoughts and emotions. No doubt from spending too much time glued to their programming boxes called televisions. It is little wonder then that you are able to catch any glimpses of the Real when your heads are filled with apple-pie junk.'

'So television is bad for us then?' I asked, thinking it was a fair enough assessment. I had never really been much of a fan of television myself; more an addict of news if anything. I always considered most television programs to be catering to the lowest common denominator.

'It will not help you if I say something is good or bad. If I say something is good, you will indulge in it, believing that you will benefit from this indulgence. Likewise, if I say something is bad, you will refrain from it, believing also that you will gain benefit from your restraint. These are nothing more than actions of blind mimicry.' There was silence for a while. Soon after this Monroe stood up from where we had been sitting under the shade of the tree, and smoothed down his trousers and stood up straight. It was time to move on; to continue our journey through the high paths that trailed across the mountains surrounding Benamahoma. We walked on; or rather Monroe walked on and I fell in step one pace behind. I had the feeling it was up to me to find a way of re-entering the conversation around television. It was as if Monroe had instigated a deliberate break in order to make me re-think my line of questioning.

'How does television, and television programming, affect human consciousness?' I asked, sensing that this was a more specific and less abstract approach.

'Well, funny you should ask that', said Monroe in a tone that was borderline mocking. 'This is a question of how one understands the nature of consciousness and the human being. It also involves how a person perceives the nature of thought, mind, and consciousness. Since we are on the subject of television, let us make this our analogy. We can say that human consciousness exists external to our physical bodies. This is not fantasy or crazy thinking, as your very own sciences have been verifying this through quantum biology and the nature of the quantum vacuum. Some of your thinkers have even discussed this in terms of the akashic field. This is an energetic field of intelligence, which exists beyond the physical. The mind is what we can refer to as the physical apparatus or organ within the body, which picks up on the external consciousness. Finally, human thoughts are what are produced when the mind interprets these external signals. For example, when you turn on the television, the television program is not inside the television but exists external to it as information that is broadcast. In other words, it is a frequency signal. The television is an antenna that picks up this frequency, and the technology inside is what translates it into pictures. In this analogy, consciousness is the broadcast, or frequency signal; the mind is the television antenna; and human thought is the picture which gets interpreted and displayed on the screen.' Monroe stopped at the crest of a hill where a path sloped down into the familiar town below us. We were almost back to where we had started – as if that were ever possible. Monroe titled his Panama hat further over his forehead. He turned to look at me squarely. 'You' he went on to say, 'are a transmitter, a frequency signal, for others here on Earth. That is what humans are

– and that is what humans do. And yet television, your great box god, is a form of *frequency control*. Entertainment is really entrainment – it lowers your frequency signal so that it operates, or broadcasts, upon a low mumble. The development of television programming is not an accident; it is a known and manipulated technology of frequency resonance. Sure, you can watch as much television as you wish – if it is your desire to remain in a trance. Too much television ogling acts as a brain sedative. You may laugh at this, yet it is they who are having the last laugh at you. You don't have to believe what I say, just go and observe for yourself. Go and enter a bar where there is a television set on display, and note how it affects human interaction, conversation, and attention. Talk about dazed states! All these recent movies about zombies – now who's having the joke? You really shouldn't let them laugh in your face like this.'

Nothing more was said between us until we entered Benamahoma. We stopped by the running fountain to drink the famous fresh mountain water that the town is famous for. We refreshed our thirst as the sound of birds filled the airwaves. One or two cars stopped by to fill their dozen or so empty plastic bottles with mountain water. Monroe turned and catching my eye he tapped the side of his head. 'Your view of the world is the view you have inside your own heads.

You are kept prisoner by your own senses and fed representations to keep you happy. Humanity is like children eagerly trying to explore their immediate environment, and pushing buttons you shouldn't be pushing.

'What kind of buttons?' I immediately asked.

'Atomic ones' replied Monroe as he turned away and walked down the road.

We said goodbye at his front gate. Monroe was smiling broadly as if greeting me for the first time. I felt a warmth inside as the sun's rays fell warmly on my back. Walking away I had a sensation of joy and fullness, and yet my mind could remember little of the day's conversations.

MEETING FOUR

I had spent the last couple of days since the previous meeting listening to the recordings I had made and transcribing them. I wanted to do this whilst impressions were still fresh in my mind. It was not only what Monroe said, but also his mannerisms, his body language and inflections. I knew I needed to add these throughout the text in the places where I thought they had occurred, or where I had glimpses of a memory. I also remembered too my own reactions and thoughts. Writing these down, as I am doing now, almost feels like personal therapy – a form of introspection!

Already I had had three meetings with the person I knew only as Monroe. There were many things I still needed to process. It felt as if he was deliberately planting seeds in me that would grow either at a later time, or at the appropriate time. Right now it was planting time. Beyond this there was little else I could grasp. It seemed a better option just to go with the flow; and to ask questions later.

The next time I arrived I pushed through the front gate and knocked gently on his door. As usual his appearance suggested that he was expecting me. Whenever I arrived it never seemed to surprise Monroe, even though it had been several days since our previous meeting. After the Monroe welcome of a wide smile and a gentle hand upon the shoulder he motioned for me to follow him outside. With a brisk pace I attempted to keep up with him as he sauntered up the road; his trademark white Panama hat hovering like an orb on a mirage of warm air. We finally stopped at a low white adobe wall with wire fencing along the top.

'What do you see?' Monroe asked with a gaze off into the distance. I wasn't sure what I was looking for. Before me was an open field. 'You still cannot see?' queried Monroe. Yet before I could answer Monroe swiftly walked on a few paces and opened a small gate in the low-hung wall. I followed him and we walked toward the far end of the field. As we approached I realized what he had wanted me to see: a row of wooden bee hives. 'We go no further', said Monroe with a motion of his hand. 'We do not wish to disturb the bees with our presence'. We both paused, and in this silence I began to hear a buzzing sound in the air. Bee activity was going on all around, yet we had to still ourselves in order for it to percolate through our senses. 'Often we only realize the work of bees when it is too late, and we are stung as a warning not to intrude further' said Monroe after the prolonged silence. 'Their work is so important, and meaningful, to human life and yet most of you ignore or trespass on their presence.'

'I've always appreciated their honey though' I replied. I wanted to say something positive to add to this unexpected conversation on bees. Monroe looked at me sideways and raised his eyebrows. 'I'm sure too that the bees appreciate your liking of their honey' said Monroe with just the slightest hint of irony in his voice. 'A spiritual bond exists between a beekeeper and the bees', continued Monroe, 'and if a beekeeper dies, this death must immediately be made known to the bees. If this is not done, all the bees will die within the course of the next year. A sense of community exists between the beekeeper and the bees - they belong to each other. There is great wisdom in the beehive and the beekeeper understands and respects this - it is a living intelligence. An individual bee is not wise, yet together the hive has a powerful and instinctive wisdom.' The bees like living messengers darted across the scene in front of us, no doubt aware of our all too obvious presence. A part of nature, they hummed and resonated with the work and play of duty and growth.

Back in the garden of Monroe's house I helped him collect a small basket of fresh herbs for our salad. Kneeling on the ground, in his agile manner, Monroe was picking the herbs so deftly I could imagine him having done this all his life – however long that had been. 'There is an important difference between questions and answers that most of you people have completely unsuspected. In a linear fashion you are programmed to ask a question and then wait only a short time for its matching answer. Yet what you have not correctly perceived is that whilst a question may be asked at almost any time and place, its corresponding answer may come at a special time and place. The two are not necessarily related according to linear time. Your linear time is a construct from your mental-rational stage of consciousness. Time for others is completely different because a specific state of consciousness perceives the energy environment differently. As your own consciousness mutates so too will you experience a morphing of time. It is already happening now; these early stages are characterized by what seems to you to be a speeding up of time; or less hours in the day to do what you wish to do!'

'And with modern technologies everyone seems to be multi-tasking, increasing their activities or being stressed from over-connectivity' I added. Monroe appeared to nod in agreement as we strolled back to his kitchen to prepare lunch.

'The rise of the internet and your global technologies are part of this emerging consciousness mutation. Increased connectivity will indeed stress the minds of some if they do not learn to balance these impacts. Communication technologies that are arising now help to foster non-linear, non-local connectivity and perception. An increased familiarization with non-local connectivity will also help in bringing you people back to a more abstract, visual and non-linear consciousness. Eventually your technologies and the human mind will shift to an ethereal stage, as materiality softens into non-visible connectivity. The wave that goes from material growth to dematerialization is a standard cycle. All stages of civilization must eventually pass through it if they are to develop past certain primitive stages. It is also important in the balancing of feminine energies and heart intelligence. Yet it is a transition stage that is both dangerous and yet terribly exciting for you.'

Preparing food with another person is a joy I had forgotten. Having lived for so many years alone, especially since arriving in Andalusia, I had become used to the act of preparing and eating food alone. With shared hands, the activity of food preparation appealed to my natural instincts; almost as if my genes stored memories of human communities surviving through this ritual. I suddenly remembered what Monroe had said earlier about the bees – the individual bee is not wise, yet together the beehive has a powerful and instinctive wisdom. It is a collective that works and dies together, and yet the hive continues over many years, even though the individual bees are constantly replaced.

'It is important that humanity recognizes it is a collective?' I asked Monroe once we had seated to eat.

'In truth I am surprised you had forgotten' smiled Monroe. 'There is so much information in your biological memory banks that you need to *re*-member that you are a member! Growth always comes through the collective – the whole – and the individual must contribute to this. Not every individual is required; just enough of those who know, and who have the power to affect change. Developmental growth requires a minimum threshold.'

'And is this the transition stage you were talking about earlier?'

'I wished to say that at such periods of change, which includes the potential for developmental growth, there are always disturbances. These are the interference patterns of different modes of reality. Imagine if you have a stone and you throw it into a pond; you get a ring of water waves that disperse outwards. You may consider these to be the energies radiating out from a particular cycle. Now imagine you have two stones and you throw them together into a pond; both radiate circular ripples, yet when they come into contact with one another they cause a disturbance. You get interference waves. As a new cycle of developmental growth emerges to replace the old cycle, their energies create interference. And that is what is occurring now on your planet. Your current reality is based very heavily upon a dogma of materiality, and a doctrine of material acquisition. This belief system will not let go so easily, so it is vying to maintain control. Yet the reality on your planet is being shifted to incorporate other levels of perception. Whilst this is taking place, which will be over quite a number of years and certainly not overnight, you will have to deal physically, mentally, and emotionally, with these affects of interference. It is more physics than metaphysics – more ecology than esoterics!' Monroe made me laugh by pulling an odd face and lifting up his hands as if in guru worship. 'Let me repeat a story to you' he continued as he delicately ate his salad. 'This story has been printed in your own books so it is nothing new – if indeed you cared to search for it. It tells of a wandering stranger who once stopped a king in the street. Furious, the king shouted – "How dare you, a man of little worth, interrupt the progress of your sovereign?" The stranger answered – "Can you truly be a sovereign if you cannot even fill my begging bowl?" And he held out his bowl to the king. In wishing to show his generosity to the crowd that had now assembled, the king ordered the stranger's begging bowl to be filled with gold. But no sooner had the bowl appeared to be full of gold coins they disappeared and the bowl seemed empty once again. Sack after sack of gold coins was brought, and still the begging bowl devoured them all. "Stop", screamed the king, "this trick of yours is emptying my treasury!" "Perhaps to you I am emptying your treasury", said the stranger; "but to others I am merely illustrating a truth". "And what is this truth?" asked the king. "The truth is that the bowl is the desires of humankind, and the gold is what humanity is given. There is no end to humanity's capacity to devour, without being in any way changed. See, the bowl has eaten nearly all your wealth, but it is still an empty piece of carved old wood, which has not partaken of the nature of gold in any respect".' Monroe poured me a fresh glass of cool water. I must have been wearing a blank look for Monroe chuckled to himself. 'Alright, a few words upon the story for our bemused guest. True reality by its very nature is more participatory than people realize. Throughout life a person must allow their experiences to create change within them, so that external impacts can stimulate an internal shift. Humans are prone to devour greedily the world around them, gorging on the stimulants it provides; yet so few are changed in any measurable way. People must become the alchemists of their own transformation. I could give you a bicycle as an aid for transportation; but would you expect me to ride it for you so you could reach your destination?'

'So if reality is more participatory it means that we should become more involved in the way we think about the world and act in it?' I asked, wishing for some clarification.

'It means coming into a more direct relationship with your external world. And this means connecting one's inner world with what is perceived to be occurring *outside* of oneself. The problem you currently have here are the interferences; the disturbances that distract you from really perceiving the nature of your reality. Some of these distractions are the general consequences, or remnants, of your stage of material life. There are other distractions which are fostered upon you more deliberately, with intent to distract. Have you not noticed that your 'modern' way of life is increasingly distracting?'

'Sure', I replied. 'This was one of the reasons why I moved out here to southern Spain. I wanted to get away from the general groove, and find a place with land where I could focus my energies.'

'Exactly' said Monroe as he wagged his finger. 'You felt the inner need to change, to shift your priorities. This is an energy that represents the new emerging cycle of growth. It requires that people are aligned with it; more in tune with its energies and needs. And if you listen to it, you too will find yourself shifting elements in your own life: your job and career, your focus, goals, your needs, and finally your perceptions of what is important in life. Yet many people are still caught up in the artificial distractions that distort you from perceiving a more subtle reality. This distorted reality that surrounds you is no longer beneficial to your further developmental growth. That is why over many years there have been elements seeded into your cultures, both mainstream and peripheral, that have served to catalyze new potentials of thinking. The changes, or mutations, in human perception must come from within. If a new reality was to land in front of you – plonk! – here today like a ready-ordered meal, it would literally blow your minds. It would certainly blow the fuses of your human nervous system. Apart from the few, perceptual grow is incremental. Reality is shifted in front of you in a way that you don't see one screen disappear and another emerge. The process is one of merging and morphing.'

'And I suppose there is a lot of merging and morphing going on right now?' I asked, half in question and half as a statement.

'There is indeed. Yet more serious to the point is that there is also an increase in the distractions – and this is not good for the collective. So there are measures being taken.'

'Measures?' I queried.

'These are not to concern you, other than to say we are speaking right now. And you are taking notes with your recorder, and from this certain factors will take their own course. What you need to understand is that it is important in these years to focus one's mind and state of being. Otherwise a person can end up confused within themselves because they are open to all sorts of external impacts that mess with their balance and harmony. These are part of the dangers of living within a reality experiencing distortion. Your frequencies are being interfered with, as if the whole planet were transfixed by a huge global television screen blaring out its programs whilst everyone stands surrounded by a forest fire.' I didn't know what to say to this. The images in my head were of people sleeping whilst the house was burning down around them. 'Now, this isn't the time to be dramatic or fearful', said Monroe as if reading – or seeing – my thoughts. 'It is a time for balanced awareness; to know more of the situation in which you find yourself. The very process of life is about broadening one's understanding of reality – and to then creatively participate in these realities. What you should be aware of is that people will by consequence naturally attract the energies that support their version – their perception - of life. Therefore, the more uncertainty you hold in yourself, the more life appears confusing to you. Collecting too many beliefs only adds to this already complex illusion…or should I say delusion?' said Monroe with a wry knowing smile. 'Look, when you truly know something, you *know* it – end of debate. But when you only think or believe about a thing, then you must be careful. You need to know you are dealing with subjective opinions, which are most likely a combination of mixed thought processes, external environmental impacts of the moment, and longer-term social conditioning. Be careful what you represent; don't go backing the goofy horse.' Monroe fell silent then and proceeded to delicately finish the small scraps of food on his plate. I had observed Monroe's eating manners over our previous meetings, and noted how he not only ate frugally, but also with a sense of grace. It was as if he knew exactly what he was eating; and importantly, how much of it he needed to ingest. He never appeared to eat more than he required, regardless of whether there was ample food still laid on the table. I began to feel almost greedy when eating in front of him. I was sure I had a greater hunger than he did. Besides, I argued internally, my younger body needed more energy!

For the first time Monroe invited me to drink an after lunch tea inside the house. We entered an interior room where it was cool, away from the warm, balmy spring sun. He left me seated in a tapestry-covered armchair whilst he went off to brew the tea. The room was sparse, uncluttered, yet cozy; unlike many Spanish homes that radiate a cleanliness close to hospital hygiene. Rather than pictures framed along the walls several tapestries hung in sequence. On closer inspection I saw that they depicted scenes of the Moors, and clearly their making had Arabic influence. They showed what appeared to be both Moors and Christians in friendship together.

'Benamahoma', came Monroe's voice from behind, 'means "Sons of Muhammad" in Arabic. This small town is well-known for its association between the two cultures and their respective religions. It is not only famous for its bees! You should be here for the festival of *Moros y Cristianos* in early August. There is more birthed here in this small town than just the source of the Majaceite river' smiled Monroe as he placed a tray with teapot and cups on the table.

'Green tea is good for the body's digestion' explained Monroe as he filled the two cups with a subtle-scented tea. 'We need to make sure our bodies are well looked after. Well, I do especially' smiled Monroe. 'You have the best designed biological machines in the universe; and you stuff them with fast food, fatty nonsense, and sit on your backsides complaining of obesity epidemics. You sure do make for amusement!'

'I'm sure we do' I agreed. 'Crazy, illogical, rationally irrational; we are a technically insane species that has learned to normalize this into sanity.'

'You said it', nodded Monroe. Then, after a short pause, he raised his finger – 'Ah, but such a necessary and unique species, no matter how insane you might appear to be.'

'Anyway, going back to what you were saying' I said, wishing to return to what Monroe had begun discussing earlier at the patio table. 'Are you saying we must be careful not to become fearful?'

'Most definitely. You have been programmed as a species to believe in your own disempowerment. Your educational and religious systems often condition you to submit to external authorities. The result is that you manifest obedience to authority over and above the necessary requirements. This repression is causing disturbances in other areas of human emotional life. It is important to realize that not only have you a right to know about yourself, but you have a right to know what it is that is stopping you from knowing.'

'And so our emotional lives are unbalanced then?' I asked, not quite sure.

'For the majority of you I would say yes, indeed, your emotional lives are unbalanced. Partly this is because of very early social conditioning which you have yet to break away from, so this is not entirely your own fault. Yet on top of this we have a whole array of entertainment industries which serve to manipulate emotional energies; often through supplying buckets of saccharine slosh. Your media corporations are adept at creating a hyper-reality that is even further from any sense of "normal" everyday reality. On one level it is a cleverly delivered form of escapism from a fearful world that their own news channels have already pre-supplied. On another level, it is a distribution of frequencies which, as I have already said, is not in yours or anyone's best interests.'

'So television and mainstream media really are bad for us then?' I said with confidence. I had had this sense for many years, and was secretly glad that this was now finally being confirmed.

'Again, it is not a question of is it good or bad' replied Monroe briskly. 'It is about being made aware of the forces and impacts in your environment. Escapism is good for a person who wishes to escape. Your terms of reference are subjective, just as are mine. As an example, my subjective opinion is that humans like to admire and amuse themselves in equal measure. And when not amusing themselves they remain in bewilderment.' Monroe smiled benevolently, yet I had the sense that behind his smile was a smirk.

'I sometimes get the sense that you are laughing at me' I said jokingly, although I had a serious intention behind the charge.

'Not in the way that you think' replied Monroe as he leaned forward to fill my cup with more green tea. 'Certainly I am laughing with you; or rather, prompting you to laugh at yourself. Without humor there is no insight. And anyone who does not laugh will be unable to see beyond the confinements of this reality. Humor is a great tool. For one it stretches the muscles and stops us from becoming a sour-faced puss. And on the other hand it helps to release people from indoctrination by disturbing their conditioning. Was it not one of your own highly regarded philosophers, Plato, who said that, and I quote, "Serious things cannot be understood without humorous things – nor opposites without opposites". That is why authority is humorless – it is a bully. Listen to this: an American tourist visits an old Tibetan shrine high in the Himalayan mountains after weeks of travelling. When he arrives an aged, shriveled monk shows him through the sacred shine and they come to a single burning flame. "This flame", says the ancient custodian, "has been burning for more than a thousand years". After saying that the American reaches over and blows out the flame and says "Don't worry old man, it's out now!".' At this Monroe burst into laughter and rocked back in his chair. I couldn't help but laugh, although more at Monroe's own joy than the joke itself. Monroe obviously found the whole thing hilarious. I sipped my tea in my own amusement as I watched Monroe roll his eyes and shake his head. Then, after composing himself, he learned forward over the table and said in a conspirational tone – "Have you heard about the Secret Teacher?".' I confessed that I had not. 'I once knew of a person who spent years trying to track down the Secret Teacher that was supposedly the Hidden Master of all wisdom on the planet. And this person', whispered Monroe, 'finally found this supposed Hidden One. "Are you the Secret Teacher?" he asked. "Yes, I am" replied the Master. "Then can you teach me your secrets?" asked the seeker. "No, I certainly cannot" replied the master abruptly, "as I have no wisdom and I don't know anything…but hey, don't tell anyone – now it's *our secret*!".' Again Monroe shook his head with obvious delight and left the room. I was left alone sipping my tea, smiling to myself in my own amusement; until a sudden wave of bewilderment came over me. Then I suddenly remembered the words Monroe had spoken only minutes before: *my subjective opinion is that humans like to admire and amuse themselves in equal measure. And when not amusing themselves they remain in bewilderment.* I had to laugh.

After a long time waiting I had the feeling that Monroe had probably left me to my own thoughts. I no doubt deserved this. Perhaps I was in danger of becoming a victim to my own seriousness! I eventually stood up and made my way into the kitchen. Monroe was not there either, yet I spotted him through the window, sitting on his garden bench in the shade. I stepped outside and, armed with my recorder, made my way to greet him.
'Not too serious', he said as I approached, 'yet perhaps too excited by curiosity. You are attracted to the magical, the mystical, and the mysterious. I know how to get your attention like this!', and he snapped his fingers.
'The non-ordinary does appeal to me' I admitted.

'Then you must take care to distinguish between the elements of an alternative reality that can be useful and meaningful to you; and the mere magician's distractions of this world. A seeker is not the same as a self-amuser' replied Monroe. I said the point was well taken. I sat down next to Monroe and relaxed amid the bird calls of the shade.

'My advice is that people of this world really need to get themselves balanced and grounded. Real changes are coming that will have the potential to affect human psychology, as well as emotions. There is also the potential that such disturbances will be amplified. A large human population emits a strong emotional frequency. If this emotion is then exploited to carry tones of fear, worry, stress, etc, then little else can get through. What you have is a frenetic emotional firewall. This then gets projected back into your framework of reality. In your world, an energetic mass created by groups of people with shared intent is a reality. It manifests in your existence and becomes real for you. You will come to understand that you *are* what you are afraid of. On the other side, you can also *become* what you wish to intend and focus on. However, it should not be reduced to pacifying slogans. Your reality is at this time being redefined; yet you are not consciously aware of this. You have some very simplistic notions currently spreading through your societies, masquerading as minimal truths. "You can change your reality"; "Intend and it will be so"; "Visualize yourself rich", etc; yet these slogans obscure more profound and beneficial truths. You have the slogans yet not the knowledge to either understand or implement these processes. You are reading a menu, or even putting it into your mouths, believing it to be the same as the delicious food it describes. You are not there yet – although you are beginning to open your eyes. What you need to be focusing on are your future potentials. Each moment in a human life affects potential outcomes. The timeline of your life is more flexible than you may realize. That is why a human life is constantly in motion – all the parts of the larger picture endlessly rearranging. Don't be static – and don't be defeatist. You need to involve some trickery here.'

'What kind of trickery?' I asked

'The kind of trickery', replied Monroe with a side smile, 'that involves confounding a current belief structure in order to perceive another. It is interesting how things are hidden in realities.'

'And so we must become more aware of our social conditioning, so we can see past the systems that indoctrinate us and which manipulate our emotions' I said, feeling confident that I had gotten Monroe's chain of thoughts.

'Yes', nodded Monroe. 'Many people here on Earth don't even realize that they are accustomed, and persuaded, into getting their information from sources which specialize in providing it – and not by individual thought, observation, or training. However, information without knowledge makes a person a prisoner instead of an escapee. The situation that has thus arisen is that many people now live within prisons of their own choosing. The prison is the person themselves, and they become their own warder as well. While the warder is the prisoner and the prison, it is not surprising that there are so few escapes, and rescues are so rare.'

'Yet we need to begin escaping now don't we? If not, we are in danger of being led down the path of wrong and misleading information by our governments. And the system, which is now crumbling around us, will never change. We have to begin bringing in our new awareness and understanding' I said.

'That is exactly so' replied Monroe with a kind smile. 'People need to be aware of the overt manipulation of human emotions from insensitive minds. And people have their own responsibility too. When you stop listening to what people say and instead observe what they are doing, you will see a different picture. Don't be confused by their words. Observe their behaviour. Then you will have more information on how to respond appropriately. Your world needs to evolve, and *so do you!*' said Monroe with a strong emphasis on the final three words. Then he stood up from the bench and began walking back to the house. 'I'll see you to your car' said Monroe as we took the path leading to his front gate.

Our talk for the day was over, and it was now late afternoon. Or rather, in Spanish terms, it was siesta time. We walked out onto the street.

'It is your responsibility to be a part of this world, no matter how crazy it seems. That is why you are all so important. You are already here, and you can affect change from within. It is not the same for us. We have to be subtle; we can influence, yet not directly play the game like you can. You need to play your part whilst being a part of this world.' I nodded and thanked Monroe for his words and his kind hospitality. As I turned to open the car door I heard Monroe call from behind 'Come back soon.'

'I will' I said. Yet Monroe was no longer there to hear my words.

MEETING FIVE

THE spring weather in Andalusia was continuing to be kind to us. My days were passing in a tranquil, comfortable haze. I was fortunate that at this particular moment I was between projects, which meant that I had some in-between time on my hands. I was also concerned about preparing and planting my garden. As always, I was plagued by the sudden subterranean invasion of weeds that sprout like armies of the foreign legion. Each day I would be out in the vegetable garden uprooting by hand these local residents. Spring was an active time for Nature, and my neighbors were ploughing and planting like madmen. I didn't wish to get caught behind; for my vegetables to miss the prime growing season. At the same time, I had another routine now. I was the unofficial companion to a person whom I confess to not knowing the slightest. The figure I called Monroe was a puzzle to me. He spoke in a way that I felt made great sense to me. And yet the mystery of our meeting only fuelled the suspicion that he was other than his appearance led to believe. His way of words gave a sense that he was an objective observer of the human race, and that he was privy to the 'bigger picture'. Beyond that I didn't care to speculate or fantasize. In truth, I was content enough just to receive and record his words. The origins of this man were only a matter of curiosity, and in that way not truly important.

I realized, and accepted, that I was within the slipstream of an opportunity that was taking me along. Of this I was greatly appreciative; and thus I considered it better to go with the flow rather than analyze and rationalize the currents of the flow. When you get it, go with it…that's how I was feeling.

I had parked the car and was walking up the hill toward where Monroe's small white house was situated. I decided to make a stop at the fountain before reaching the house, to take a few handfuls of the delicious mountain water. After all, Benamahoma was well-known as the source of the river that flowed into the larger Guadalete River, named after the Arabic for the "River of Forgetfulness". I hoped that my few small handfuls would not lead to any amnesia. Perhaps, I imagined, the whole of humankind had drunk in some way from this river, and we were now a world asleep.

Vague remnants of some unobtainable memories clung like driftwood to the back of our minds. And this irretrievable sense of knowing kept us just barely awake to continue with our lives. Knowing we once had known something is like an unreachable longing that dwells deep within us throughout our lives. Such contact never leaves us, yet lays like a slumbering serpent awaiting the spark for its awakening.

   Refreshed, I walked on and rounded the curve in the road to begin the second slope of ascent. As I did so I heard an immaculate English accent float through the air like a feather dart: 'Going somewhere young man?' I turned around to see Monroe sitting on the terrace of a restaurant, smiling broadly at me. I smiled back and raised my hand, half in a gesture of being 'caught' in some hide-and-seek game. Yet again, I had been surprised and, more to the point, smoothly out-maneuvered. Monroe remained seated as I joined him at the table and pulled out the recorder. I ordered a cold tonic water, with lemon, and observed Monroe gazing out down the road. He must have seen me coming from halfway down the road, and watched me as I drank from the fountain. It was the ideal vantage point to observe all human and non-human traffic. I was observing the observer, with the feeling I too was being observed in some unsuspected, nonlinear way.

'Meetings are rarely what they appear to be' said Monroe after the waiter had set down my drink. I said nothing and waited for him to continue. 'Encounters fall into different categories; some of them may be for a specific reason, whilst others are part of the hustle and bustle of a life in motion. Encounters can sometimes be meetings, yet meetings are never mere encounters. One should learn to discern the difference.'

'And what we have is a meeting I suppose' I replied, also gazing out down the road.

'No suppose about it. It very definitely is.' There was a long pause as neither of us spoke. I was becoming comfortable now with the silences that intervened in our conversations. I had come to realize that the silences were as much a part of the conversation as the words. They were like silent words that came to bring harmony and balance into a caravan of sentences.

'Communication is continuous and unbroken, and functions ceaselessly. Everything is in communication – constant communication. Nothing is in isolation; that is how this universe works. Your species has forgotten this. There are distant memories of this bonded communication lurking in you somewhere. I expect you have stuffed it away somewhere amidst your 95 percent junk DNA' Monroe said grinning. 'Well, whatever you have done with it, rest assured it hasn't left you entirely. It just leaves your *sapiens*

sapiens "doubly knowing" species not very communicative. So we have to hobble around with you too. As the saying goes, "In a village where everyone only has one leg, the biped will hop about more lamely than anyone else, if he knows what is good for him!"' At this we both laughed, and brought our glasses together in a cheerful 'salud' for good health.

'I hope we don't make you too uncomfortable here?' I asked

'We get by. Or as the English are so keen on saying – we mustn't grumble! It is only a matter', said Monroe fixing his gaze on me, 'of maintaining functional and operative channels of communication. Ideas and potentials must be seeded ahead of their time in order, so to speak, to prepare the mental ground. This is why there is a deep sense of separateness on this planet. Not because there is no vibrant, communicative life in the dimensional aspect of your universe; but because you have been kept incommunicado due to your unpreparedness in encountering – and meeting – these other realities of life. The universe that you are aware of exists *for you* in relation to the capacities and potentials of your perception. We can state this in a more fanciful way by saying humanity has, thus far, been kept in perceptual quarantine through sense-deprivation.

'But why?' I asked, now feeling a little perplexed.

'The reason being is that you are not yet ready; not en masse anyway. So there is a trickle-down process in place. A few individuals are suitably developed – or 'trained', to use your vernacular – to be able to cope with receiving finer perceptual inputs. These suitably developed individuals then operate within your own cultures to seed and disperse required information, piece by piece, and often ahead of time. These ideas, or call them impacts, then through various channels make contact with human consciousness to slowly prepare humanity for the full transition. It is an evolutionary process that can be referred to as *incubation*: one stage of evolutionary development is activated whilst still inside the current civilization's womb. Each epoch has its evolutionary mutants. Many of them have been famous in your history – and most of them for all the wrong reasons! And yet so many more have gone unnoticed and unknown, as befits their work best. Fame is, after all, quite a distraction.

'And so how do we develop as individuals?'

    'By need', replied Monroe.

'And do I have the need?' I asked, feeling a little awkward at such a direct question. Monroe smiled.

'Not if you have to ask like this' he said, raising an eyebrow. Monroe ordered a small plate of locally prepared grilled vegetables and croquettes for the both of us. Then he called the waiter back (purposely I felt) to make a deliberate show of ordering two beers. I smiled when Monroe had finished making the order. The thought of a cold beer was definitely on top of my list. 'Well', said Monroe as he leaned on the table across from me, 'there is no use being here if you cannot enjoy a few delights along the way.'

The cold beer was refreshing as I took a long first gulp. 'Got to keep the energies up!' I exclaimed as I sat back in the chair. I felt a sense of appreciation for not only having these conversations with Monroe but for the fact that I could be sitting here, in a small town amid the splendor of Natural park mountains, free from stress whilst the world shuddered on around us. 'Not a bad place in the world to be', I continued, feeling relaxed and contented. Monroe just nodded his head.

'Sure, not a bad place to be – yet not without reason of course'

'What do you mean by that?' I asked.

'Southern Spain – Andalusia in particular – has played an important part in the cultural transmission of developmental energies.' Monroe cracked in half a crusty fried croquette and examined closely the contents. 'Spinach', he noted in an agreeable tone.

'What happened in Andalusia?' I prompted.

'It goes back to the twelve century. A specific projection – a phase in cultural transmission – arrived, or rather was seeded, in Andalusia as a gateway to help develop the western world. This projection established many of the impulses of creativity that, centuries later, assisted in the emergence of the western Renaissance. This, for example, is one crude example of the way certain operations work. Cultural flourishes almost always have their origins much further back at some specifically seeded developmental impulse. Your historians are largely unable to recognize this due to their narrow-minded, or perhaps I should say "select", way of understanding cultural transmission. One thing they do seem to agree on, more or less, is the pattern of cultural cycles, which is indeed the case.'

'So we should be looking at culture and human development in terms of cycles then?' I asked.

'This would be a good start' agreed Monroe. 'Human development is deeply linked to universal cycles. When there is a particular energetic cycle in your cosmic neighborhood there are specific opportunities for evolutionary development. This applies to humanity as well as it does to Earth, the solar system, and beyond. When the "cosmic winds blow", so to speak, certain processes are placed in operation. Galactic cycles have been known about and observed on this planet for eons. Many of your past known civilizations have famously utilized this, not to mention many great civilizations still unknown to your mainstream history. It is unfortunate that in your so-called "modern civilization" - or is it *post-modern* nowadays? - I forget the correct parlance' chuckled

Monroe, 'such cycles have been trivialized, and reduced to low-level entertainment so their true effects and influence are little known to the masses. The macrocosm is translated into the microcosm through various means – such as astrology. It is regrettable that astrology is now viewed mostly as gossip column trivia for bored housewives – which in most cases it is due to lightweight career seekers. Yet there are real codes to be found in there. The universe is full of codes for those who know how to look. It has its own fingerprints – specific energetic signatures. That is how it communicates, like an energetic Morse Code: dot dot, dash dash, and a little dash more…. A dash more beer?' I looked down at my glass and realized I had supped it dry.

'Thirsty work listening to you' I smiled.

'Thirstier work still to be done' replied Monroe with a raise of his eyebrows. We finished our tapas as the sun shifted across the sky overhead bringing light into our once shaded terrace. I made my leave to visit the bathroom, as it was my plan to also pay the bill. Yet when I came to ask for the bill I was told by the waiter that the 'distinguished gentleman' had his own tab that was taken care of and I didn't need to pay. There was nothing I could do to remonstrate. I walked back out onto the terrace to find Monroe already gone. I looked around, wondering if he had somehow slipped past me to visit the washroom. I walked over to our table and retrieved my digital recorder. It was then that I saw Monroe on the street below, admiring some flowers in a ceramic urn.

'So many things right in front of our eyes' said Monroe, opening his hands palm upwards to the sky.

'I suppose all we have to do is look' I said, wishing to affirm his statement.

'No' replied Monroe immediately. 'All we have to do is open our eyes.' He pointed to a small bird not far away; unusual looking with a colored crown. 'Do you know what bird this is?' asked Monroe. I shook my head. I had no idea. I was sure I had not seen this type of bird before. 'It is called the Hoopoe. You often see them in Andalusia. There has been one in my garden every time you have visited. Pity you never had the eyes to see it before' said Monroe with his now characteristic sideways glance. I pursed my lips and nodded my head. 'The hoopoe bird has an interesting literary history...you should *look* it up sometime' continued Monroe. I agreed that I would.

We walked together up the main street of the town. Monroe pointed out to me the dedication to the friendship between the Christians and the Moors, and how we were actually walking down the 'Christian and Moor' street. We turned up a bend and approached a small whitewashed church that had a dome-shape look to it.

'Yes, it is noticeable' pointed Monroe. 'This building was a small mosque before the Christians acquired and converted it...same energies though; and similar function.' We stepped inside to where the air was cool. A few small rows of pews were arranged in front of us. I followed Monroe as he made his way to the front to sit down. 'You people are really *hard work*' said Monroe as he leaned slightly over to me.

'What do you mean?' I asked.

'Well, you just don't seem to want to know about how to develop. You behave as if the concept does not exist; when in fact it is the most natural and normal thing in the whole universe! Instead you tell yourself so many rubbish stories and create a human mythology more cardboard than the Three Wise Men and more childish than Peter Pan. Your scientific interpretations of the universe have made life boring and meaningless for you. This is not wholly deliberate of course, although partly so. The belief in a dead universe is a form of controlled indoctrination. It completely alters how you view reality, and severely limits your possibilities for developmental growth. You humans believe things too readily. Just because a person in a white lab coat says something, or you read it in print, does not necessarily make it true. You exhibit a conditioned response to authority – often a blind obedience. You need to change this state of affairs so rather than being full of implanted suggestions that you accept as true, you need to begin accessing and acknowledging your own intuitive truths.' Monroe leaned away and then quickly leaned back again to continue. 'You have been told so many stories – narratives within narratives – that you are swimming in a murky sea of beliefs. You are in the world during a time when belief systems are crumbling. Systems by definition also require systems-busters' said Monroe as he gently patted my shoulder.

'Why aren't we whispering?' I said in a whisper.

'You are; I'm not' replied Monroe. 'Perhaps you haven't realized it yet, but there's nobody else here…and nobody's home.'

After exiting the small church we walked through the empty bull ring that stood nearby and continued until we reached what seemed to be the edge of town. Taking a path down from the road we began walking along the base of Benamahoma along its perimeter.

'When are you going to smell the bath salts and wake up?' asked Monroe after a few minutes of walking in silence.

'I really don't know' I replied, thinking that he was talking to me personally.

'Well, it's coming along fine!' he grinned, as if to let me know I should not take anything on a personal level. 'There are plans within plans within plans. There has to be when you are dealing with something this complex. All the interrelated levels have to move in relation along their potentials. This particular universe progresses through ever increasing levels of complexity. You have heard of entropy?' I agreed that I had. I explained to Monroe that I had a background in the complexity sciences, and that I had been heavily involved in this subject at university. 'Wonderful!' he said, showing delight. 'Nothing is for no reason – if you will excuse the double negative. Well, as you are so keenly aware, entropy is basically the law of decay; when something moves from a greater to a lesser energy state, yes?' I nodded my agreement. 'Good. And so for the universe not to decay it is required to keep on processing available energy into greater levels of matter-complexity to a point where there is the maximum potential for coherence amongst all its parts. This includes atoms and their spinning electrons; to living bodies; solar systems; galaxies; and the universe to which these laws apply - all evolving towards optimum coherence.'

'And what happens when that optimum coherence is reached?' I asked.

'Good question. Well, it is the end of a cycle. All matter returns to its primary state of energetic non-matter. And another cycle begins, like a new wave bursting forth from the ocean of everness.' Monroe looked over at my perplexed expression. 'I should not worry about this; we are discussing time lines well in advance of your ability to conceive. Yet what it does tell us is that impulses of energy are required at specific junctures – at precise time windows – in order to catalyze development beyond a moment of potential decay, according to entropy. Here on this planet you suffer from the natural cycle of decline. No terrestrial organization or individual can resist this process of decline. This is why those who know this set up institutions and projects that are designed only for a limited effective life. In brief, developmental impulses exist for a specific moment, at particular locations, in accordance with known local factors. After a time, the impulse is no longer functional, and decays. It is a primitive habit to wish to worship the remnant; which unfortunately occurs quite a lot on this planet.'

'You mean in terms of worshipping ideologies and beliefs?' I asked.

'Belief systems, ideas, monuments, institutions, locations, trends...the whole smorgasbord.'

'Is that our human habit to cling to what we know?'

'That, as well as clinging to the outer forms and structures. You fail to appreciate the kernel when you worship the shell. For example, you manifest a belief system that tells you the universe *as you perceive it* must be how it is. Yet this paradoxically shows a complete lack of perception. That which you honor as your scientific belief system suffers greatly from this flaw. Your human science is based upon your sensory perceptions, which we have noted are limited and subjective. Have you not yet realized that the parameters used for the visible are unable to prove the invisible? And yet your scientific establishment insists on making judgments about that which you are unable to see. Just because you cannot perceive something does not mean that it has no existence or meaning. Your whole lives are in fact based around invisibles; not least your assumptions and speculations.'

'Perhaps we are afraid of that which we don't know?' I said somewhat in a defensive tone.

'Part of your fear is understandable as it comes from the conditioning on this planet; and within this current epoch especially. The other part is a lack of necessity in pushing out the parameters of your perceptions. In this matter you may be pushed into a perceptual shift from factors outside your control.'

'Such as?'

'Such as the juncture – the time window – I previously spoke of' Monroe said as we arrived at the beginning of the town, having come full circle. Monroe stopped walking and placed his hands on his hips. He gazed at the view surrounding us in full panorama before producing a loud, satisfying exhale. 'Ahhh...*We shall not cease from exploration, and the end of all our exploring will be to arrive where we started and know the place for the first time....*' I raised my eyebrows and stood in silence. There was no way I could follow that! 'T.S Eliot, my dear fellow' said Monroe under his breath.

Monroe sat down at a café table near a small fountain-come-roundabout that marked the road entering the town. It was the first time I had walked through Benamahoma with Monroe, and it felt both a little strange as well as comfortable. I had always experienced Monroe within his own environments, whether it were his house, garden, or his secluded mountain walks. Today I was seeing a more social side of Monroe. I was somewhat surprised to notice that almost everyone who passed seemed to know Monroe. They invariably all said hello and raised their hand in greeting. Even the waiter at the café knew Monroe in a familiar way, and brought his cup of hot green tea without waiting to be asked. I requested the same, not sure what I felt like drinking. Tea, or rather green tea, seemed better than most options.

'It is difficult to imagine, let alone conceive of, universal evolution when one is sitting in such a tranquil and beautiful part of the world. It is like being in the central fulcrum of the universe here, where everything is still and all motion proceeds around this centre. We sense very little here; yet the energies allow us to perceive much of what is occurring around us.' I remained silent, not feeling any need to respond. With my digital recorder a silent witness I was just another pair of ears. 'Universal cycles are so grand', continued Monroe after a sip of his tea, 'that their time frames are perceivable to so few. Multiple universes come into existence constantly, almost as if birthed. Do you realize how finely tuned this current universe is?'

'I'm not sure what you mean by finely tuned' I replied.

'It has been said by your own scientists that you live in a "Goldilocks" universe; that is, conditions are "just right" – neither too hot nor too cold. The exact combination of push-and-pull forces, combined with the precise quantity of specific gases at the birth of this universe are so minutely exact and precise, it is a wonder. One of your own mathematical physicists has calculated that the probability of coming across such a universe, fine-tuned to life, by random selection is 1 in $10^{10^{123}}$. With these odds it appears you would have a better chance on betting that a living universal intelligence exists!' smiled Monroe. 'And I am quoting your own science.'

'So how did the universe come to be so finely tuned at its inception?' I asked. This was a new subject for me, as I had never been well versed in the astronomical sciences.

'They expand and pop just like balloons, over and over again' said Monroe as he made a pop sound with his mouth.

'Blow and pop – now that's novel' I replied, hoping to sound somewhat tongue-in-cheek.

'More or less' replied Monroe with a slight grin. 'Each universe goes through its own evolutionary cycle; as it does so it gathers a collective memory. The universe is itself a unified field of energy – and intelligent too. When the end of its cycle is reached, which is usually maximum coherence – although maximum chaos has also been known – then it reaches an inflexion point. You might call it an explosion-implosion moment. A new universe is birthed from the mother sea of energy, and each new universe retains the *memory*, so to speak, of previous universal cycles. Each cycle learns from the previous one. No universe manifests from nothing. This is why your universe is so fine-tuned – it emerged having acquired all the information from previous cycles. The constants were already known.' Monroe finished, looked at my blank expression, and chuckled. 'Perhaps baby universes is just a little too much for you' he said sympathetically.

'Maybe' I agreed. 'Yet is there a connection with anything going on right now?' I asked.

'There is' confirmed Monroe with a serious nod. 'There are moments in expanding cycles where certain "jumps" occur, almost like the interval in a musical scale. These moments coincide with particular energy movements that affect certain cosmic neighborhoods. You are in it right now. It is similar to what your evolutionary biologists refer to as "punctuated equilibrium", only that it occurs on a larger scale. These moments of potential evolutionary expansion may, by some, be referred to as upgrades; although I myself prefer not to use this term as it comes with too much human baggage – if you know what I mean?'

'So this expansion is going to affect us, or is already affecting us?' I asked.

'Yes. And it will continue to do so over some time. The ideas, structures, and belief systems current on this planet are going through, and will continue to go through, great change. This change, in evolutionary terms, will be rapid. For you, it will be only a few generations. In fact, you are already seeing the changes within your own generation. Generational shifts are noticeable for you because the human physiology changes, thus affecting the nervous system and human perception. Yet time constructs are not accurate in describing the context of this change. You realize that time is a construct that is relevant only within the context of your reality; it is thus not fixed. The notion of relational time is, for the most part, informed by the rhythms and cycles of your fellow planetary bodies in this system; and, of course, by your great sparkling sun-star. For planet Earth particularly, the moon is a major factor in your rhythms – biological, mental, emotional – and so has a lot to answer for. We have not yet secured the correct functioning of the moon; yet this is a subject for another time. It is worth noting also that time for you is seemingly accelerating because your perception of time is altering. This is also due to the impact of your technologies. There will be considerable electromagnetic change also that will affect your environment, and to some degree your individual human energies. You will need to adjust to this. Those who are born later will arrive more adjusted, as the incubation period in the mother's womb, as well as their initial years of life, will provide the necessary signals for their physiological adjustment.' Monroe finished speaking and emptied his cup of tea. 'Yes, I know' he said with a gentle voice; 'it is a lot to take in. Yet do not worry, there is nothing to fear. You need only to open-up to your own opportunity to evolve. It can be a lesson for you also. You can choose to what degree you participate and learn from this process.' Monroe turned to look at me and I picked up a shimmer in his eyes. His stare was direct and steady yet, I felt, sympathetic also. 'I should also say' he went on, 'that there is simultaneously a movement to create fear and confusion on this planet. You should not concern yourself with this, nor respond to it emotionally. Be aware of its presence; yet be neutral, and remain balanced and positive. Do not play into this game – it is not *your* game. Be aware of those in your world who wish to bring you limitation; yet listen to your own authority. Work toward an expanded view of reality. Don't stay confined. Remember that in your world you have certain agreements about reality. These serve to anchor you, but should not restrain you. Be grounded and balanced, yet also visionary and creative. Embrace possibility and potential.' Having said this Monroe rose to leave. I grabbed the recorder and got up from my chair.

'I'll just go to pay' I said. Monroe waved me away with his hand. 'No need dear chap. It is already sorted; he is a friend of mine.' Monroe gave one of his charismatic smiles followed by a friendly wink.

I was tired yet exhilarated when I returned to my house. I had lots of weeding that needed doing in the garden. I stepped inside, plugged the digital recorder into my computer, and collapsed onto the sofa. In the shaded coolness I fell quickly into a Spanish siesta.

MEETING SIX

THE tiredness of the previous day had gone, although I felt overloaded as if pumped with too much information. Being in the presence of Monroe was most of the time comfortable and relaxing; yet there were moments when he opened the tap and so much seemed to flood into me. I was sure I was unable to store it all, let alone make adequate use of it. I considered myself a recorder – a librarian – or a witness perhaps. I also had within me a sneaky feeling that there was something else occurring during our meetings. It was hard to explain though, or put into a picture. It was as if Monroe, by talking of these things, was catalyzing another operation. I had a sensation that something was happening within this time frame, within our reality, through the act of these seemingly innocent conversations. I knew it sounded rather grand, or even 'mystical'; yet it was just a sensation I had. Neither had I given much reflection to our actual encounter. If I were to speak of this to others – even thinking of it as I write this now – sounds so uncanny, so unreal. And yet the whole thing to me was so natural I hadn't even blinked. In fact, I had continued to meet with Monroe as if he were an old friend, when in reality I knew nothing about him. Even now I am unable to question this. I return home and often transcribe our conversations by typing them out into these pages. I have not yet had the chance to really scrutinize what he has been saying, or even evaluate them. All I can say is that it all makes sense when I am with him; although upon returning home I forget much of what was said. Then in transferring his words to the printed page I am so focused I do not absorb the significance of Monroe's words. Perhaps when it is all finished I will sit back and read through all I have written – and 'know the place for the first time'. I just wanted to say this – here and now – before I go on to transcribe our next meeting. I felt I had to say these words in case any reader thinks me incredulous or gullible. All I can say in my meek defense is that I'm not being naïve, nor intentionally misleading. I'm here to pass on some words, some message...and I'm just going with the flow.

***

It was a 30 minute drive to the town of Benamahoma from where I lived. The road was a good one; a modern road that ran straight over the plains toward the rising peaks of the Sierra de Grazalema Natural Park in the distance. Little houses dotted through the fields littered the view from both sides of the main road. A few *ventas*, local restaurants, also sat along the road to attract passing trade. Usually such places offered good food and low prices. Just over halfway on the route I would pass by the exit to the small town of Prado del Rey. This small sheltered town was well-known for its weekend markets and local food. I sometimes visited Prado del Rey on a Saturday morning to pick-up some organic vegetables, when my own garden stock had finished, or withered away. This was a familiar route to me. Yet now I was reminding myself to be more aware, more mindful, of my habitual passing. I wished to note the skyline, the colors of the fields, and the clouds across the mountaintops, on each journey to Benamahoma. Otherwise it would all be the same, and each passing would merge into one until the separate tastes were unknown.

I passed through El Bosque, the town before Benamahoma, and took the left turning onto the winding mountain road that began the final five kilometer inclination to the small town where the sons of Muhammad mingled with the bees.

I parked the car as usual yet instead of going directly to Monroe's house I preferred once again to first walk to the fountain where taps in the long wall were gushing with the fresh mountain spring water. With cupped hands I took several gulps of the crisp, refreshing water and savored its taste. It was hard to believe that reality could be an illusion – or delusion – and yet be so real at the same time. It seemed as if this was the paradox: our reality is both so real for us, so finely tuned to our states of perception, and yet so close, less than a hair-width away, from other realities and dimensions. It was as if humanity were standing on a thin bridge, a human foot wide, and on either side of this bridge stretches out unbelievable new worlds and vistas. Yet we are both unable to either perceive these vistas or move beyond the foot-wide berth of our passage. Unknowingly, our lives are shuffled along this thin spectrum of perception, our literal footbridge, from one end to the other. Time, I felt, to begin peering sideways as we crossed. I crossed the road and walked a little way to the familiar white house where Monroe lived; or rather, to where he was residing. I could not be sure neither how long he had lived there nor how much longer he would remain. These, until now, had never been questions that had arisen. I brushed away these questions, for I felt they were not important or relevant. All that mattered was that Monroe was in this place for this time. Other considerations would have their own valid and appropriate contexts.

    I had the impulse to go around to the back of the house rather than to knock on the front door, as was customary. I wasn't sure if this was conscious intuition or complacent familiarity. Either way, I passed through the front gate and took the small side path that wove its way to the garden at the rear of the house. The first thing I noticed was that the table on the back patio had already been prepared, and had its plates and glasses neatly arranged, with napkins folded awaiting its hungry guests. I looked around and found Monroe to be seated on his shady garden bench with a pad in his hands. As I approached I noticed that his attention was fixed on the landscape that spread out past his garden fence and into the far distant hills. Monroe himself was the epitome of summer elegance. His white linen shirt was pristine, as if ironed by an invisible hand, and his white trousers were spotless. The characteristic white Panama hat was perched on his head, and his clean-shaved almost-youthful face was calm and focused. I sensed that behind this elegant exterior sat a boyish energy and playful humor. Monroe threw me a quick smile and winked before returning to his concentration. The cheeky chap was reading me like a book, I was sure of it. I sat beside him and peered discreetly at his pad. Monroe was sketching the vista with only a graphite pencil. The accuracy and detail of his rendering was astonishing. I was taken aback with surprise. It was akin to the work produced by autistic savants. Every nuance of the scenery had been picked up by Monroe's keen eye. I nodded my head in approval, not that Monroe needed or expected my approval. He pursed his lips.

'Mmm...not bad; but still rather rough' he murmured under his breath. I had to laugh at this blatant understatement.

'It's more than not bad Monroe – and you know it!' I said with half a laugh.

'Why would I know it?' replied Monroe in a serious voice. And then after a pause added, 'what may be good enough for you is not necessarily the same context for me. It is extremely subjective to make a judgment based only on one's own limitations, wouldn't you say?'

'Yesss' I agreed, a little disheartened. 'Still, I think you draw pretty well.'

'Pretty well!' exclaimed Monroe with a look of feigned shock. 'What is well and pretty about it? And is your *pretty well* any better than my *not bad*? I think it is better to draw than talk like chickens with these sloganisms.' We both looked at each other straight-faced. Monroe laughed first and patted my shoulder. 'Lighten up soldier!' he said chuckling. 'You're not a chicken yet....'

After a few minutes of silent appreciation of our surroundings I commented on how elegant he looked today, as he did always when we met.

'Elegance is an appreciation of the self' Monroe replied. 'It is a measure of respect to be, what you would say, *presentable*. We each must choose our manner and form of negotiating with life. If we are careless and dirty with ourselves, the world appears careless and dirty to our own perceptions. It is a matter of correct perspective – of intentioned organization. We must respect ourselves, if we wish to ask the same from the world that is our reality.' Monroe looked me up and down, in an obvious deliberate manner so I thought, and tilted his head whilst letting out a 'mmmm' murmur. 'You yourself are smart enough. You show you have respect for yourself. You are not a lazy person – although too many people are. If you wish to engage with the world, participate with your reality, you should present yourself for it. You should be saying – "Look, here I am. I'm ready for you. I'm prepared to negotiate with reality. You can work with me – I'm committed". In this slippery world you walk through, it is important to be impeccable. Don't give reasons to your detractors. Neither be an excuse for yourself nor an excuse for others to use against you.'

'You're talking like we should be warriors' I replied.

'That's right soldier – head up, back straight!' said Monroe in a tone mocking a drill sergeant. 'Warriors of a kind' he then added, smiling. 'And why should you not be? If you are not a warrior within then you have fear. Fear is one of the most dangerous things for people. Fear pulls a person further into the trap of your reality and lessens your potential for perception. Fear is a wonderful distracter; it keeps you occupied on the mundane, and on the false.'

'And what are the other dangerous things?' I asked as we sat down at the table to eat.

'Self-doubt, of course' replied Monroe almost casually as he poured me a glass of water. In a sudden flash I realized that in all our meetings it had always been Monroe who had arranged the table, provided the food, and even who served me. Although I was the 'guest', in some loose way, I could at least have been more generous in my attitude to serve. This sudden realization flushed me, and I felt so guilty – and greedy. Monroe flicked a quick glance my way, yet said nothing. We began to eat in silence. I looked away to hide my embarrassment. For several minutes Monroe didn't even look at me, yet I knew he was watching, observing everything. I discreetly saw as he picked up a slice of cheese, looked at it from all angles as would an architect, and then gently place it in his mouth. He closed his eyes as if savoring the taste. He didn't open his eyes again until he had finished eating the cheese. Then giving me a direct look he asked, 'Are you here to be spiritual?' I froze. I wasn't expecting that question. I had no idea what to say. 'Well?' said Monroe prompting me.

'No' I replied. It was the first answer that came to me. Luckily for me too it felt genuine.

'That's right' said Monroe nodding. 'It is better to be normal first. You have a funny story in your culture that tells of a spiritual seeker who, after finally finding a spiritual master that he feels is genuine, asks the master if she will accept him as a pupil. "Why do you seek a spiritual path?" asks the teacher. "Because I wish to be a generous and virtuous person; I wish to be balanced, mindful, caring, and to be in service for humanity. This is my goal" says the seeker. "Well", replied the teacher, "these are not goals on the spiritual path; these are the very basics of being human which we need before we even begin to learn".' Monroe chuckled to himself and gave me a wink. I felt better immediately. We continued eating in a more light-hearted mood, with Monroe telling me a little about the history of the Moors in Spain, and in Andalusia especially.

'A long, observed history of growth and development' said Monroe finally. 'Quite impressive, like we said in one of our earlier talks. First humanity walked across the lands, and then you opened up land trade routes to connect and trade with other groups and tribes. Before long you were building your ships and floating off down canals, waterways, seas and oceans to expand your precious trade routes. Then with great human innovation you took to wandering the airwaves in your tin planes. This really helped to change the human psyche and perspective - great distances in such short times. Yet this wasn't enough. Humanity had to dive past the Earth's atmosphere and jump into space. Human eyes for the first time in your known recorded history viewing your precious planet from outside...Wow! Now, what else do we have?' said Monroe with upturned eyes. I was sure he was making some mock display with me. 'Ah yes, the rise of the alphabet made linear script and rational consciousness more prevalent, finally birthing a left-brained dominant culture that is logical and linear. Mmm...although now your modern global communications - the internet, the Ethernet, the wonder-net!' exclaimed Monroe waving his hands almost comically, 'are pushing forth the abstract into human minds. Well, is there hope that more and more of your human minds will operate in left-right brain wholeness? You know soldier, a little more empathy and participation in the larger world around you, kind of thing' said Monroe with a raise of his eyebrows.

'Could be' I said, half-jokingly, half serious.

'It is all about acquiring the correct tools for bringing in the appropriate state of consciousness and perception' said Monroe, in a way that subtly shifted the tone of the conversation. 'Decades from now, even less I suspect, you will have a whole new range of vocabulary to deal with the mutation of your consciousness. You are struggling now to frame these emerging experiences as you currently lack the vocabulary to adequately express, and thus project, these new perceptions. Circumstances are overtaking you. Your old language models are not sufficient to describe what is happening, and also what is about to happen. Yet these are natural, organic, evolutionary changes. You need to understand that evolution upon the Earth occurs in relation to the evolution of human consciousness. And you are reaching out for the stars.'

Monroe raised his glass of water in a toast. We clinked our glasses together. A dog barked in the distance.

'Will we ever reach the stars?' I asked, knowing full well this was little more than a bridging question.

'Humanity is already a part of the stars' replied Monroe with a slight shrug. 'What is needed now is for you to bring this into your reality and into your everyday mass consciousness. You know that!' said Monroe with a smile. He was goading me somewhat now.

'Sure' I replied, taking the bait willingly. 'It's all about preparing for a change in human consciousness over the years to come.'

'Exactamente' nodded Monroe. 'Consciousness defines how your world appears to you. The world you have today is a product of your human consciousness. You have created some wonderful imaginings about your pre-historic past. You have museums piled high with the reconstructions of your deep ancestors roaming the planet three and a half million years ago - and of the dinosaurs stomping around - yet you are viewing this scene from the consciousness of today. This consciousness was not existent at that time, and so the world was not as clearly defined then. The solidity you have today is a direct reflection of your more refined state of consciousness. This is the mistake you doubly wise sapiens sapiens make today' Monroe said with a slight inflection of irony in his voice. 'You observe everything through your lens without realizing the observer affects the observed. You are separated, cut off from the larger reality because your split consciousness defines a clear separation from object and observer. This was not always the case in your far past. Your ancestors participated much more with their environment because, like new born babes, they could not clearly perceive a solid separation between the self and the other. I keep telling you that everything is a matter of perception, my dear fellow.'

'Yet I expect that change is coming; hence these conversations' I said.

'Indeed that is correct. And you can assist in this process by understanding that consciousness does not exist in separation from the world. It participates with the world as waves do within the sea.

Human consciousness, for most of you, separates and splits your sense of reality. It is not that humans no longer participate with the reality of your world today; it is that you are not aware of perspectives beyond your conditioned boundaries. It is intriguing and yet alarming to observe how many of you sleepwalk your way through what you call a "life". It is a prison without bars, so you will never attempt to escape because you are unable to perceive your own predicament. Sometimes to walk amongst you folk is like moving through a world of the living dead. Sorry if it sounds too blunt for you my dear soldier.' Monroe sat back and drizzled some olive oil onto a plate of salad.

'So, we're collectively suffering from a case of zombiefication. I can relate to that' I said. 'Yet what I now need to know is what can we do about this situation?'

'A pragmatic response; that is good' Monroe replied with a gentle wag of his finger toward me. 'Despite what I have been saying you might think that humanity made a mistake by severing this intimacy with a participatory reality; yet this is not entirely true. The separation was…mmm…well, if not entirely planned, then let us say it was encouraged.' At this Monroe smiled. 'You see, to forever dwell within this state would eventually stunt the development of individual consciousness. So it was necessary that a separation take place for the evolution of individual consciousness to take hold.

There can be no true unified group soul if the individual elements do not have their respective awareness. So the hope was that humanity, manifesting a consciousness of separation, would eventually develop this into a conscious participation with reality, thus returning to this state yet on a higher level of perception. Do you grasp the significance of this?'

'Not exactly' I said, 'although I think I grasp the general gist. So we are to evolve our consciousness to once again reach a point where we are in participatory connection with our particular reality?'

'Yesss' Monroe said with a look that told me it was more or less so. 'Only this time when you return to a living, participatory immersion with reality, you will do so from an individual, conscious position. This awareness of how you exist within your reality is crucial; for without conscious awareness the next level of evolutionary growth cannot occur. No more can your species be blind, lacking perceptual vision.

'Yet do you feel we are ready for this?' I asked, wondering aloud.

'If you are not given the opportunity to grow and develop, then you will never be ready. Humanity cannot remain as spiritual pigmies within the cosmos for ever!' remarked Monroe with a soft, warming smile. I had the feeling that despite everything, Monroe actually had a deep compassion for all living things.

'So we need to be ready for this new understanding then, this new perception of our part in an evolving cosmos?'

'Yes, you *do* need to be ready' said Monroe with strong emphasis. 'Yet with understanding comes responsibility. The impact of the human mind upon the world is a very real physical phenomenon. The future of the human imagination will influence the future physical aspect of planet Earth. The freedom to have individualized consciousness is a great freedom indeed. It must be used wisely and with aligned intention. At the moment this is not entirely the case...' Monroe paused. 'Well, we can say for now that there are measures being taken to counterbalance these disruptive influences' he added with a wink as he rose from the table. I waited several minutes for Monroe to return, as I wanted to ask him what he meant by counterbalances. I had assumed Monroe was going to the kitchen to fetch something; or perhaps even a visit to the bathroom. I think I must have waited a good ten minutes before the penny finally dropped. I rose from the table and entered the salon in the house where Monroe was reading a Spanish daily newspaper – upside down! Yet he appeared to be reading and understanding it as if he was reading normally. I was getting a little more accustomed to Monroe's displays, so I knew it best not to react to this. He was, for sure, prodding at my impatient curiosity.

'Okay', I said, 'you got me. So - may I ask what these counterbalances are?'

'Oh yes, you may ask' replied Monroe. And he went back to reading his upside down newspaper. I went and sat in the chair across from him.

'Alright then – what are these counterbalances?'

'Finally, a more direct question!' said Monroe half-jokingly as he folded his newspaper. 'Unfortunately, I must be somewhat vague with you on this one. It would neither be appropriate to, how you say it, spill the beans; nor to overly-feed your impressive curiosity. Further, of course, I have to speak according to your capacity to understand these concepts; and in this regard your capacity is lower than the range of facts I could convey. However, I can say that there has been an exact science operating in the world for as long as modern humans have existed. This science has been maintained throughout your various cultures and civilizations by those elements I have referred to as counterbalances. Most of these counterbalances have gone unrecognized because they do not fit the description of peoples' expectations. The shining enlightened spiritual figure, gliding softly on sandals, draped in bleached, crinkle-free robes, is more a product of your own advertising agencies than it is of reality. In your history the real counter-forces have operated anonymously. And not only that, but such work on this planet has been unpopular with other outside forces for a long time. Circumstances can be made difficult here for certain operations to function. That is why operations of a developmental kind have been disguised as normal processes within your own cultures; dressed within the rituals, costumes, and customs of the specific local environments of their operation. There are two kinds of developed beings on this planet who work with such developmental operations. There are those who come from outside to perform necessary tasks; and those who are developed on this planet from among ordinary humans. These latter sometimes have long, publically known lineages; other times they are singular, unknown persons who live and die upon this planet without ever being suspected or known by the public. Such work as undertaken in this regard has been vulnerable to double risks. First, as I just said, from outside hostile forces opposed to this work. Secondly, by human physiological weaknesses that affects the functioning of the human body. Performing the necessary work can lead to an accelerated deterioration of the human body and nervous system. Certain human flaws can become exaggerated under these conditions. A high-profile example of this is the person you call your Christ. In reality he often walked with a limp, and was a smaller, dark-haired man who knew how to play the fool - and not the tall, handsome figure from your history lessons. Of course, all references to this fact have been deleted from known records. Although the religious depiction of a saintly "village idiot" and "simple-minded pilgrim" are vestiges of this truth. Of this I will say no more at this moment of time. What I am giving you is baby food – so that it is easy to digest. I will tell you something different at another time: as you change, the story changes. The state and presence of your own being will determine what you understand. You carry the codes within you for opening many of the doors that lay ahead. You are your own adventurer.' Monroe finished speaking and rose slowly, yet gracefully, from his chair. He motioned for me to follow him.

Standing in the middle of the garden at the rear of the house we both gazed up at the sky. We were like star-gazers during the spring day sunshine. The heat warmed us but did not burn or make us uncomfortable. The sun shone behind us as a few clouds danced above.

'Do you see the stars shining out there?' asked Monroe in a soft voice.

'No' I said. 'I see only brightness....brightness and light.'

'Why not?' asked Monroe.

'I know they are there', I replied, 'yet my eyes cannot see them because they are shielded by the light.'

'And can you perceive them'?

'No' I said. 'I cannot.'

'Cannot what?' queried Monroe.

'I cannot perceive them.'

'Not yet.'

'Yes, not yet' I agreed.

'You are at the right time to start making choices.' Monroe put his hand on my shoulder arm as he passed and returned to the house. I did not follow. I had the feeling that everything had been said for today. And, besides, I still had the rest of the day to deal with…so much to do. I felt rejuvenated.

MEETING SEVEN

THE morning was dull and overcast on this particular un-spring-like day. Until now we had been blessed with a glorious early start to the coming summer. I expected that the high summer months this year in Andalusia would be another hot one. I had been behind in my spring planting, although I had managed in the few days before my first meeting with Monroe to plant some young fruit trees. Now that the daytime temperatures were high enough I had planned to plant some grass seeds in the wild area at the back of my house. First though, I had to prepare the soil. Thinking of this, over breakfast, made me recollect a phrase that Monroe – I believe – had once said casually when we were not recording. It was something like the need to prepare the mental soil in advance of the actualization of ideas in order for them to become accepted mental currency. It went something like that…according to my memory.

Such words had all been forgotten at the time, only sparked into life now as I was thinking about my own actual garden planting. There were many things Monroe had said that were 'outside' of our recorded conversations. Most of these remarks were casual, almost 'off-the-cuff'. Yet with everything that Monroe said, there was a significance buried behind the words. On more than one occasion he had even hinted that much of this information would lie beyond reach for the time being; waiting to be actualized by specific life experiences, or triggers. Sometimes these triggers will come naturally through a person's own process of development, Monroe had said. Other times, the triggers will be activated by specific targeted impacts – what this meant I was unclear. All I can say at this point is that I have been provided – or rather, I feel I have been given, or gifted – more than I can either remember or use at this moment. Like seeds planted during spring; they grow when the right amount of light, heat, and water are provided. Sometimes this comes organically through the hand of Nature; other times it is provided carefully by the gardener's hand.

It was with a sense of gratitude and appreciation that I remember driving to Benamahoma that particular morning. It was to be my seventh meeting with Monroe. How time was passing! And yet it felt so 'un-right' (this was the only way I could express this) to think in terms of time. I had the odd inner sensation that I truly did not know who Monroe was – in any shape or form - and also that I had somehow known this 'person' for ever. I was thankful for these 'lunchtime conversations' between us, and yet also mindful that they were both for a reason, and for a certain time. And I say that these conversations were 'between us' when in fact it was more truthful to say that I was receiving these conversations rather than acting as equal partner or participant. I had to smile at this. Besides, it was only my ego that had once persuaded me to consider our conversations as mutual exchanges; when it simply wasn't the case. A hazy sun began to drizzle through the cloud cover, bringing light to what was to become another fine spring day.

Walking casually from where I parked my car to Monroe's little white Andalusian house my attention was drawn inward. I was thinking about the range of questions that had built up in my mind during the drive here. I thought it was about time to ask more directly about Monroe himself – his background; his reasons for being here; and his future hopes and expectations. Although a part of me realized that these were perhaps more selfish questions – or ones based on satisfying curiosity – I felt it was important for me to know the answers to such questions. In this frame of mind I stepped through the small hinged gate and, almost automatically, followed the path to the back of the house. I was expecting to see

Monroe seated as usual at the prepared lunch table. Or perhaps he would be seated at his bench under the tree in the garden…or pottering about with his flowers. All these images came to my mind, and began conjuring a set of familiar scenes to greet me. Yet I was greeted by nothing upon my arrival. Or it would be more accurate to say that I was greeted by the absence of presence. Monroe was not to be seen, nor heard. There was a perceptible silence to the garden that I had not noted before. Even the birds seemed quiet, as if it was an off-chirping day. It took me a few seconds to fully register the certainty that Monroe was not here, and that today would not be a day for our conversations.

I moved around to the front of the house, walking slowly, a little unsure of myself. I had mixed feelings inside: a combination of deflated expectations, unwanted surprise, dry humor, and a hole waiting to be filled. I was about to turn toward the gate to leave when something on Monroe's front door caught my eye. As I began to approach I saw that there was a note fixed to the door. I walked up close and read what had been left:

1. Information without knowledge makes a prisoner instead of an escapee

2. Hope of improvement is not a substitute for capacity to improve

3. Do not think that your magic ring will work if you are not yourself Solomon

4. See you next time

The meeting that was not a meeting had given me something at least - perhaps more than a whole conversation would have. I took the note and smiled. Oddly crazy but so true.

MEETING EIGHT

'**AH**, what a delight' said Monroe with a broad smile as I approached the table. 'You know, I do enjoy our conversations. It would be a shame if at this point we were to miss any, don't you think?' he said without the slightest irony in his voice.

'Sure, me too' I replied smiling back at the elegant figure of Monroe. Again, I could not help but admire the impeccable way he presented himself, even within the walls of his own home.

'The self is what we can talk about today; if you will permit it?' asked Monroe with a gracious tilt of his white Panama hat.

'Of course, a good subject for me' I agreed.

'Fine, then it is agreed. The self, by its very nature, also includes society and culture, and, well, the whole universe too!' grinned Monroe. He had me again. The conversation, as on previous occasions, could go in any direction Monroe so wished. 'Do you know the bird of paradise plant?' asked Monroe as he strolled down the steps into the garden. I replied that I did not, as I followed behind. 'Correctly speaking it is called *strelitzia reginae*, although people like myself prefer the plumage-sounding title; it is much more regal. And here it is' Monroe said as he made a sweep of his arm to show me a firm green-stemmed plant that had beautiful, somewhat ornate fiery orange petals that could be taken to look like a bird's head and colored crown. 'A wonderfully ornate specimen' mused Monroe, as if speaking to himself or no-one in particular. Then, on turning to me, widened his piercing blue eyes – 'low-maintenance and functional' he said in a calm and measured tone. 'Loves the sun, grows in almost any soils, and assists the process of pollination. An all-round beauty she is. And apart from her magnificent blooming, the rest of the time she is incredibly discreet, and hardly noticeable. She does her thing, remarkably well I would say, and then gets on with being a low-key marvel. She would fit into any garden, and would not require much of the gardener's hand either. That is important: the ability to blend in tactfully at the same time as contributing something important and necessary to the overall garden culture. Are you hungry?'

'I'm okay' I said, noting how Monroe had abruptly changed the topic of conversation.

'I'm sure you are okay' said Monroe with a raise of his eyebrows. 'I was not asking about your general well-being – although thank you for the update. Now, are you hungry?' Monroe stood stone still, evidently awaiting my response.

'Hungry enough to eat and listen' I said, hoping to be truthful as well as diplomatic.

'Good' said Monroe. 'I know you only come here for a free lunch' he smiled, and began walking back to the house.

I had the impression that Monroe was observing me more acutely than normal. There were moments, during our casual lunch and chatter, where I caught him peering at me (I say peering, although if it were anyone else I would perhaps call it staring). On a few occasions I would meet his eyes and return a smile. As was the custom now, after a few minutes of general small talk – about Spain, the seasons, the regional vegetation, etc – I would place the digital recorder on the table, and Monroe would then shift the conversation to 'other' subjects. This time when I placed the recorder on the table between us Monroe raised a single eyebrow as though questioning the act. I looked directly back at Monroe, not knowing what to say. Monroe nodded to himself in silence.

'There is much still to come' Monroe finally said, his mouth slightly turning up at one side. 'And yet there must be balance…and timing.

Without correct timing there is disorganization. And within the simple complexity that is life, disorganization is not effective.'

Monroe finished saying these words and sat back in his chair; he appeared to be inwardly following some thoughts.

'And what is the significance of this?' I asked, wishing for Monroe to explain more; or at least unravel this cryptic comment.

'What is occurring is a change in human consciousnesses' said Monroe as he looked at me directly. 'Yet at the same time it is important that human emotions are not pumped up, like putting hot air into balloons. Over-emotionality can be a great weakness when this overrides the balance of human perception. Indulgence in curiosity too is a danger, for it is nothing but a selfish indulgence. This is similar to the strong desire some people have for doing good – what you sometimes refer to in your culture as the "do-gooders". Yet the greed to do good is still greed. Likewise, the greed for information is still greed. It is important to supply the nutrient without feeding the greed, or the desire. Do you understand this?'

'I think I do' I said after a pause. 'Information sometimes only feeds people's curiosity rather than assisting in their development. It is important then that people know how to use information in a way which is more perceptive...Well, that is what I get from this.' I looked at Monroe for his reaction.

'Yes', agreed Monroe. 'And the correct digestion of information is dependent upon three very basic, yet fundamental principles – these being right time, right place, right people.'

'And do we have these three principles now?' I asked.

'If you are asking whether these three factors are in operation in relation to our meetings, then the answer is yes' replied Monroe.

'So we are lucky then?' I said smiling. Monroe did not smile back this time.

'It has nothing to do with luck. It would be more accurate to say that we are fortunate.' After I did not reply Monroe smiled across the table from me and handed me some cheese. 'This is Payoyo cheese. It is an organic goats' milk cheese produced in the nearby village of Villaluenga. Go on, try it – it is delicious.' I took the hard cheese and ate a piece. Indeed, Monroe was right, yet again!'

'I do not wish you to be overly curious about how the universe operates' continued Monroe as he also took some of the Payoyo cheese. 'It can be useful background information for you, in order to provide more context; yet until you are able to perceive and fully understand it, this information can only be theoretical for you. Hence, you should not overly dwell upon it. Much of what came before has been preparatory and necessary for laying the groundwork. Can you appreciate this?'

'Yes' I replied. 'It is the same with planting; first the ground needs to be prepared so it can better receive the seeds. Without this preparation – good soil, nutrients, right season – the seeds are less likely to grow. Or if they grow they will either be weak, or at least not grow to their full potential.'

'The seed metaphor is very apt' agreed Monroe with a smile. 'And so like Nature, humanity too has a growth cycle and development potential. There is a constant influx of the need for evolution that flows through humanity. This enters all the time. Conscious individuals need to take hold of this force. It is the responsibility of humanity to extend its own tools of perception. Further, this is an opportune moment in your species life as there is literally no better time than the present to begin breaking your old perceptual patterns. Let us say, for simplicity's sake, that it is now timely. That is, the evolutionary impulse is making its presence felt quite strongly within humanity. This impulse upon the Earth facilitates the changing of old models. During this period it will be easier to break away from ingrained patterns; especially those that are mental, emotional, and behavioral. In such periods, it is possible to undergo radical re-patterning and to develop perceptual capacity. There are many developmental triggers embedded discreetly within your physical reality; these can be as subtle as flower arrangements, everyday objects, geometrical designs, or as grand as majestic monuments. Be on the look out for patterns and signals that draw you in, and for any subtle bodily reactions to encounters. That which is afar also dwells within.' Monroe began to chuckle when he saw the concentration upon my face. 'Of course', he said wagging a finger in my direction with a grin, 'there is no benefit, or use, in trying to make everything fit one pattern. There will be ever-greater anomalies coming your way. They will push and pull at your structures of reality, and gradually loosen them. Observe the pattern emerge – and help others to see it also. Don't stick rigidly to your conditioned beliefs. It is time to begin shedding these past structures, to be a part of guiding the change in, and to help prepare your fellow humans. At the same time you should also be careful not to go around stepping onto people's programs.' Monroe paused to pour himself a drink of water or, as I suspected, to create a space in order for the last point to sink in.

'And what programs are these?' I asked, knowing full well this was expected of me.

'As I have already said' continued Monroe, smiling at my "correct" question, 'each person is full of conditioning – mental, emotional, physical, and spiritual. People take things personally, and are offended if you say or do something that pushes the buttons of their programming. Most of the people most of the time tiptoe, ballet dance, or stomp through these endless programs that they encounter in a life's time. Observing this is like seeing a pinball machine game, bouncing from one impact to the other. It is a life of rebound and reaction - mixing comedy with tragedy - automation with the old spark of ignition or re-cognition. If there is no intervention there shall be chaos. If intervention is not subtle there will be madness. It is a procedure and process of caution and concise knowledge. Nothing can be left to chance – not in this topsy-turvy reality. Therefore those that begin to perceive have a duty to share what they know. Perception is a question of functionality and responsibility, and not of selfish possession. If the force of evolution moves through you, then what are you going to do with it? Humanity currently benefits from an unprecedented level of physical interconnectedness that is an external manifestation of an inner reality. The technologies you have are a mirror of your internal potentials, and function as an earlier stage of this development. You must expand upon this current state of global connectivity to develop, contribute to, and benefit from a growing empathic relationship with others. Communication, cooperation, and consciousness all work together. Have you heard of the wondrous milk of the marvelous cow?'

'No' I replied, smiling back at Monroe. I had a feeling he was on a roll right now, and that the least I said to interrupt his flow the better.

'Well, in terms of truly delicious milk, beyond a doubt there was none other like this amazing cow. The milk it produced was of such high quality, and in such great quantity, that people came from far and wide to see this wonder. The cow was praised by all, and stories of its milk production were told by parents to their children. Even teachers spoke of the marvelous cow in their classes, and preachers influenced their listeners to emulate this in their own ways. Government officials too would look toward the cow and its milk production as a paradigm of efficiency and focus, hoping they could copy this for their own societies. Everyone, it seemed, was enamored by the wondrous milk production of this marvelous cow. Yet there was one feature, however, which most people failed to observe - too absorbed were they in their adulation. This so-called marvelous cow had a habit, you see. And it was this: as soon as a pail had been filled with its wondrous milk, the cow kicked it over!' Monroe laughed as he took a sip of his water, evidently enjoying the story's finale. I found myself laughing along with Monroe in what was an infectious humor. Yet I had no idea what to say, or how to respond to this. I found the story amusing, to be sure, yet I wasn't sure what it was Monroe wanted to say by this. Monroe raised his glass in a toast: 'To capacity', he said. We chinked our glasses together in good humor. 'And why is that?' asked Monroe, in what was obviously a rhetorical question. 'Because we each need to have the capacity to make use of our gifts' he continued. 'And with this capacity we also have the responsibility to contribute to our world, or worlds. Without this involvement within the bigger picture we are as if quarantined. We are each called upon to be productive members of our society (whatever the society), and to fulfill our social obligations. Once we have fulfilled these obligations a person is ready, and able, to devote time to working on oneself. Then', said Monroe with a direct look into my eyes, 'the journey is about evolving into a multi-dimensional reality and identity.'

We cleared the table together and Monroe stepped outside as I offered to wash and clean up. A small radio stood on the kitchen counter. I turned it on to listen to some music while I washed the dishes. A flamenco voice came wafting through the airwaves; it was passionate, intense, yet with an energy of separation, of longing. The singing pulled me in and grabbed my attention, as my hands mindlessly - without authorship - did their washing duties.
'Ah, the voice of the inimitable Camarón de la Isla' said a voice. I turned to see Monroe standing at the door of the kitchen, his white Panama hat in hand as if ready to leave.
'Who?' I asked, not recognizing the name.
'Camarón de la Isla', repeated Monroe, 'the finest figure of nuevo flamenco; the bard of San Fernando. He was from this province of

Cadiz; a local voice, and a local life to be sure. Now, when you are finished we can take a step outside. These legs were made for walking!' grinned Monroe, and he raised his hat in a salute and stepped out back into the garden. I finished cleaning up, and turned the radio off as some gruff male voice replaced the hypnotic tones of Camarón.

I walked alongside Monroe as he strolled leisurely down the main road, tipping his hat and saying *buenos días* to those whom, it appeared, knew him. There was something about the fluidity, the ease and lightness of Monroe, that had always impressed me. There was nothing "heavy" about him - if I can say this? I can't really find any other words to adequately express this. There was just some lightness about the guy; and it made it incredibly easy to like him. In english we often say that a person is a *likeable fellow*; yet this wasn't it, not entirely. There was an air about Monroe that enabled him to navigate, or rather move through, life. He knew exactly how to deal with people, his mannerisms were spot on, and his reactions seemed...well, I suppose *conscious* is the best word to use. I was watching Monroe closely as we passed the restaurants at the bottom of the road and joined the path that followed the river. Several fig trees over our heads were beginning to sprout the early buds of fig fruit. Some flies buzzed in the shade as we moved out of the sun;

and the rush of water filled the air with a positive feel. We passed an old ruin that lay enigmatically embedded in the tentacles of weeds and deep beds of grass. The empty windows looking restful as two birds flew through on some gay spring chase.

'That used to be a mill' said Monroe pointing to the ruin. 'A relic from the past when mills were common here; you can find them dotted around the Andalusian landscape.' Monroe turned to look at me, 'and since you are living here for now, you perhaps should learn more about your environment. Ever thought there is a reason why you turned up here in Andalusia?' he asked.

'Perhaps it was fate' I said casually, not believing my own words. 'Perhaps' replied Monroe; 'yet not likely. Fate is what happens to people who are not attentive enough with their lives. You, my dear chap, have been quite attentive. There is no call for such humility right now!' I gave a shrug, which was perhaps a mixture of mild embarrassment and humility. 'Being attentive is what draws circumstances to a person in this reality. Yet by this I do not wish to mean that you simply create reality by your thoughts – this is commercial fodder for quick demand-supply minds. Real attention is a work in process; and it is actual work too. In developing one's presence – a *gravitas of being* – a person finds that reality responds in an altered manner because the physiology of the person is wired slightly differently. And this is what will be important about the generations yet to be born on this planet.' At this last comment my ears pricked up. I fell in step beside Monroe as we followed the winding of the river. The narrow footpath climbed over rocks and crossed a small bridge to the other side where the path continued. We continued walking in silence together until I could resist no longer. With the recorder tucked in my hand, pressed to my chest and thus closer to Monroe, I ventured the obvious question.

'What will be important about the generations to come?' Monroe didn't answer immediately as he stepped down from the path toward a small clearing where the river eddies were strongest and created a vortex where the water gathered. Little fish-heads poked up upon the periphery as the current was pushed through a narrow part of the river. Circular swirls curled and darted through the eddies, until finally consumed into the fabric of the water. I went to stand beside Monroe, and my senses were infused with the presence of the rushing river.

'Breathe. Just breathe those refreshing ions' Monroe said as he made deep inhalations. 'Like a breath of fresh air this Earth will be home to new minds and new hearts – the hope for the future. Do you have hope for the future?'

'Sure, of course I do' I replied truthfully. 'I've always been positive about the future. I realize that change takes time; and usually it comes from the periphery first, whilst the centre tries to maintain its ground and holds onto the status quo. Each epoch has its flat Earth – round Earth moments.' Monroe nodded to this in agreement.

'Quite so. These are the markers of what your scholars have called "punctuated equilibrium". They show the sudden jumps when a system increases its inflow and storage of energy before it then reaches a moment whereby it can either implode or shift into a more energy-complex system. Apologies if this sounds all too technical; I am constrained by your own language after all.' Monroe gave me a look of what could perhaps best be described as sardonic frustration.

'No, it's all right' I laughed. 'I get it. These are the stops and starts of evolution. And, from what I have picked up from you, it is during these moments when increased energy enters the system that great evolutionary leaps occur.' Monroe was listening as he picked up a small stick and tossed it into the water, watching it whirl through the small cascade. 'And so we are at such an evolutionary moment now?' I asked. Monroe turned and, for the first time, gave his thumbs up and winked. It seemed such a youthful gesture that I couldn't help but give out a laugh.

'It must be the negative ions affecting your porous head!' exclaimed Monroe smiling back. At that moment a small black dog wagged its way down from the path to where we were standing and brushed itself against Monroe's leg. Its head, which seemed too big for its semi-sausage-like body, looked up at Monroe and its big ears flapped like a bat's. Our new little black friend then sniffed at Monroe and gave a little whine before it sat down at his feet.

'Looks like you've found a new friend' I joked.

'Who said he was a new friend?' said Monroe with a straight face. I shrugged and walked over closer to the both of them.

'Well, you make a fine pair anyway' I said.

'Yes, indeed we do. A fine pair indeed' agreed Monroe. The dog gave a short, low bark and put its chin on the floor.

'And so this evolutionary shift moment we are in has something to do with the new generations being born?' I asked, hoping to continue the conversation and knowing how Monroe liked to use his pauses for effect and temptation.

'Yes it does. It is because during such periods there are increased energies made available for Earth and for processes upon the Earth. It is not important for us to go into detail about the wherefores of this energy; suffice to say that your sun gives you more than just light and heat. For you the sun is a creator energy, and a transmitter for this solar system. The sun both creates and receives its energy, which is then emitted in phases and degrees for specific processes. Increased *energized energies* are being received onto this planet. It is affecting your physical natural processes, biological processes, and the energetic signature of the planet. New generations of species, including humanity, will be born over time not only with mutated nervous systems, but also into an energetic environment that is slightly different. In fact, the two go together and function mutually. In your case, this will stimulate the emergence of a new form of human consciousness. Yet I repeat, it will not happen overnight. In terms of evolutionary time, it will be rapid and quite phenomenal. Within your human perspective it will occur over the coming generations. This change will then affect human culture, innovation, technology...well, the whole gamut in fact. It will be something worth being around for. And many will wish to be around for this too...it has been in the works already for too many years.' Monroe turned away from the water and gave me a casual smile. 'You see, humans are so impatient. They wish to see change yesterday. They believe they are the drivers of change on this planet. Yet they are blissfully ignorant of the bigger picture – of the evolutionary picture. It is a complex scheme, involving players and participants at many levels...many dimensions in fact. It is not just the case of "man discovers fire, develops technology, changes world, develops civilization, worships various gods, end of story". No, the story is much richer, much more diverse, and wonderfully creative. It is like you have been viewing your understanding of life through a pinhole. And this is what will change, as your new consciousness widens the diameter of this pinhole. Then you will encounter new realities. This might very well blow your minds; but it will not blow *their* minds. And so your generation, my dear fellow, will act as the bridge between the old and the new. And as the bridge you will have to be grounded and stable as the disruptions of change and transition manifest in your reality. You can – and you must – handle this. Welcome to your responsibility: welcome to being here.' I looked down at our little black canine friend; he lifted up one of his bat ears, and his large brown eyes peered at me.

'Why isn't there much talk about this? Are people not aware of these changes?' I asked Monroe. I was sure I had heard something similar to this on the Internet.

'There are various sources discussing these probabilities already; various sources with varying degrees of accuracy. What is of importance is that these changes are not trivialized or turned into mushy new age crystal children swinging pendulum profanities' said Monroe with a sigh to the sky. Little bat-dog barked in agreement, and Monroe and I both chuckled. One thing Monroe did not suffer from was mushyness.

'And will our future generations really be that different Monroe?'
'In time, yes they will. The difference will not be external in terms of physical shape. You are not going to be dissipating into 5th

dimensional ethers as light beings any time soon – sorry to disappoint you if you were hoping for a free ethereal ride. A significant shift will occur in your capacity to access energetic fields. Every human already has the ability to access the information field that is the base foundation of your reality. This has always been the case. You have often referred to it as receiving inspiration. This is the realm from where ideas often materialize when in fact you are accessing a vast living database. You exist as part of a living library. Once this access and organization of information within you becomes more fluid and balanced – and accepted – you will then have the keys to navigate your reality, and beyond. Let us be clear on this: inter-dimensional reality is an inter-locking whole. And on the whole these connecting influences are unperceivable to you. Your actions and behaviour may appear to you to operate in isolation, in one plane of reality, yet all actions - and thoughts - branch out to affect multiple realities. You have to adapt to new possibilities and new potentials. The old world is behind you, and humanity must acknowledge that a new unfolding is taking place, as it always inevitably does within evolutionary growth. In past centuries the human body and brain worked hard to attune to and interpret cruder impulses and influences. That epoch is now passed and humanity is receiving finer, more subtle influences. Whereas people have become accustomed to derive their sense of self through their personality, in the future they will increasingly learn how to perceive with direct knowing. This new epoch, and the centuries ahead for humanity, will be guided by imagination, inspiration, and intuition. In your future there will be no more Napoleons or Caesars; the strength of human deeds will come from the strength of the spiritual impulse working through humanity collectively. There will be a gradual shift away from speculative knowledge – your institutions of science – and toward a reality where you will increasingly draw your inspiration from an inner gnosis. A new evolutionary impulse for humanity is upon you. As another example of this shift, your various societies have long maintained a lineage in the teaching of wisdom traditions based on a teacher-student relationship for the most part. This will soon not be the case as people will begin unlocking the secrets that lie dormant within themselves. You will *learn how to learn* from accessing yourself. You will begin polishing the bridge to your Self – yet you need to take this responsibility back for yourselves. And as I say, it will not arrive overnight. These changes will come through many processes that require their own time and place to function. Part of this entails moving beyond a collective human short-sightedness that is hampering you from a correct developmental path. The myopic vision of the human species is both caging you and making you cagey. The parameters of your perception are in need of shifting – and that is exactly what will be taking place over the generations.'

'Are we really that short-sighted?' I asked as we stood at the river's edge.

'Only in relation to your current state of perception' replied Monroe matter-of-factly. 'If you were able to perceive that your reality is symbolic – that time is flexible and only appears to be linear within your dimension when in fact it is not – then you would not be as closed-minded as you are today. Earth's past is littered with the fragments of a long unsuspected human presence; as well as a long galactic presence. It is a deep shame that you do not yet know, or even suspect, your own past.' Monroe turned around and clasped my shoulder. 'Time for our return' he said and moved away. 'Come on Fuko' he called, and the little black dog jumped to its feet and trotted after Monroe like an old friend. I took another quick look at the small clearing we had been in. It seemed to me to be a beautiful spot, shielded by the overhang of the trees, a soft scent I could not recognize, and the invigorating rush of the water's journey. I said a quiet thank you to this place and left to join Monroe on the path.

The three of us took a brisk walk home. I was beginning to sweat by the time we had reached the top of the incline close to where Monroe's house was situated. Monroe stopped before we reached the bend in the road and pointed to the water gushing from the local fountain spring.

'I think you need a refreshing drink for your exertions' he said with a wicked grin. Monroe, for all his supposed age, was not showing a single tear of sweat. His skin looked supple yet somehow suitably aged, as if well-crafted. 'Come on, let us drink together' he urged. We cupped our hands and took the chilled mountain water into our mouths. 'Ahhhh...now that is better!' exclaimed Monroe. Then, as if wishing to get one last point across before our meeting's end, Monroe stood erect and eagle-eyed me. 'Look young man, what goes on in this reality is Intelligence trying to find itself – whether through fear, chaos, opposition; or through unity and compassion. These are all various aspects of the same game that is playing out. You need to be a conscious game-player, which means getting yourself on the playing-field rather than allowing yourself to be subdued on the sidelines. Be a bridge and be a game-player!'

Monroe gave a cordial salute and walked off; the little bat-eared one followed, wagging his short-cut stumpy tail. I splashed some of the chilled water onto my face. I felt intense and energized inside. It felt like a fantastic day, and I wanted to do something for the world.

    I returned home determined to be more focused with myself, and prepared for any changes yet to come.

MEETING NINE

THE Sunday morning sun streamed through my partially opened curtains to rest across my bed. 'Busy old fool, unruly sun' I said, remembering the words of the poet John Donne as he ranted against the sun rising. In my case though, I welcomed the bright and light intruder. I immediately reflected upon what Monroe had said about the sun being our energy generator and evolutionary engine. So I thanked the sun for shining, for waking me, and got up to make breakfast. Usually my Sundays were spent reading books and working in the garden, yet today I had a different urge. Or call it an itch, a nagging; a feeling inside that morphed into a knowing sense – an intuition perhaps?

I knew I had to go and visit Monroe today. Why this was odd was because I had never visited Monroe on a Sunday before. Something in my conditioning had always respected Sunday as a time of rest; a time to leave people alone unless they asked specifically to be harassed. Yet this Sunday morning I just knew I had to make a visit. Also, I drank a cup of black coffee at breakfast – another thing I don't usually do in the mornings. I'm not a morning coffee person - I'm a rooibos tea person. I guessed there had been a glitch in the system overnight.

 I checked through the world news on the Internet, like I usually do at breakfast, only to discover the general range of the tragic, the absurd, and the irreverent. It really did appear as if the human race were living in some form of quarantine, where good sense and intelligence had been taken from us and replaced by fool's gold and tinfoil hats. A part of me wanted to bang my head against the refrigerator door and watch as all the magnets came crashing to the floor. Luckily, this was only a very, very small part of me. The 'rest of me' shook its head and sighed. Yet like I had said to Monroe the other day down by the river, I was a positive person who kept a positive view of the future and of human affairs. Somehow, I always sensed that I didn't have any other alternative. I am, and always have been, what you would call a *buscador* – a seeker, a searcher - and the ways of the world had never yet satisfied my need for genuine answers. Perhaps that was why Monroe just happened to have 'bumped into' my life. There was a lot more I could say on this, yet this is not my story – it belongs to Monroe. After all, I only wanted to be a good enough bridge for the time being.

I pointed the car in the direction of Benamahoma and the bees, and headed toward the mountain peaks. This regular route took me past the roadside *ventas*, Prado del Rey, and through the town of El Bosque that sits at the edge of the Sierra de Grazalema Natural Park. As the road wound quickly through the sleepy town of El Bosque I was just about to take the left turning onto the mountain road for the 5 kilometer trek to Benamahoma when suddenly I caught something in the corner of my eye. It was a figure in white standing a few feet back from the road. I took a quick double-take. Yes, it was none other than Monroe, dressed in his characteristic white slacks and immaculate white shirt. He raised his Panama hat in greeting. I turned the car around and pulled-up to where he was standing. It was then that I noticed by his feet sat our little black canine friend from the river. I let down the window and peered out. 'Monroe?' I must have sounded surprised for Monroe gave a chuckle and bowed gently.
'The very same' he said in a diplomatically mocking tone that made me smile. 'Well then, are we getting going, or are you happy to sit in your car like a modern-day bird watcher?'

'Sure', I said, 'hop in.' Monroe opened the passenger side door and called out 'Fuko', whereupon our *salchicha* friend jumped up (barely), and lay down behind the seat. Monroe climbed in and said 'straight ahead' pointing with his finger. I followed the main road which led us not toward Benamahoma but in the direction of the larger town of Ubrique. Monroe sat comfortably in the car, gazing out at the passing scenery, a relaxed smile on his face. He had said nothing about our 'unexpected' Sunday meeting, and so I decided to say nothing of it also. I had forgotten to turn off the radio when Monroe had stepped into the car, and only now I realized this as a familiar tune caught my ear. I reached for the radio to turn it off, thinking it rude to have the interference. Monroe raised his hand – 'It's alright, you can leave this one.'

'Yes?' I queried.

'It has some lines I like' said Monroe cryptically. I tried to listen intently as I kept my eyes focused on the road. I recognized the song as a 70s one from some male singer-songwriter whose name I couldn't remember. It had a pleasant catchy rhythm, then about halfway through I noticed one of Monroe's fingers lift up slightly from his lap. I listened hard for the next line, and I heard: *Well nothing that's real is ever for free/And you just have to pay for it sometime*.² I guessed that was the line he wanted me to hear – it was *so* Monroe.

Before reaching Ubrique Monroe motioned for me to take a left turn and to follow a winding road higher into the mountains. The scenery from the road was spectacular as we drove at increasingly high altitude. After several more kilometers I realized we were approaching a small town nestled against the side of the mountain range. Sure enough, we passed a town sign that spelt out 'Benaocaz'. At Monroe's instructions I pulled off the main mountain road and immediately parked the car in an open space.

'We are going to be following the Romans this morning!' exclaimed Monroe with a wide grin.

'How's that?' I asked.

'Just across lies the ruins of an old Roman road that takes us straight – that is literally straight – down the mountain valley. If the legs are walking straight the mind has more freedom to wander.' Monroe stepped out the car, followed by Fuko, and crossed the road toward the field. I followed quickly, knowing that Monroe would not wait for slow legs (or for slow minds for that matter).

---

² Later back at home I looked up the song. It is called 'If It Doesn't Come Naturally, Leave It' by singer-songwriter Al Stewart. The whole verse goes: *Well nothing that's real is ever for free/And you just have to pay for it sometime/She said it before, she said it to me/I suppose she believed there was nothing to see/But the same old four imaginary walls/She built for living inside.*

Luckily for me I am not a general flip-flop wearer, so my soft training shoes were ideal for this path which was stony yet more or less even and easy to tread. I walked in-line beside Monroe, impressed (or rather shamed) by his physical agility.

'We are lucky in that we have a straight road today' said Monroe as he pointed ahead of us. 'Yet the immediate future will not be so straight. Nor will it be the smoothest ride in the theme park either. There are perspectives and there are perspectives…and what do we have in the middle?' Monroe turned to me with a look that suggested it was not a rhetorical question.

'Perspectives?' I said meekly. Monroe shook his head.

'Rather it is perceptions. In order to get from one earlier set of perspectives to another set we require the correct balance and capacity of perception. And for humanity, I would say this is extremely important. I might even say it is crucial.' Monroe stopped and turned to face me. Fuko sniffed in the undergrowth, his little stumpy tail wagging excitedly. 'Remember what I told you about the two stones in the water and the interference ripples?' I nodded my head. 'Well, as I said before, the energies of evolutionary shifts cause interference when there is a transition period. This energy is not negative in the sense that it is part of the catalyst for dynamic changeover. However, for those – let us say *beings* – that are caught directly in the interference patterns, there is turbulence.'

Monroe cocked his head to see if I had been following.

'So we have turbulence ahead?' I said, in what came out sounding like a question.

'Yes Captain' replied Monroe, 'we have some turbulence ahead.'

As we walked together I was trying to work out if there was a reason why we had come this far from Monroe's house. In all our previous meetings we had either stayed in his house or at least at some walking distance away from it. Now, however, we were a good car ride away; and, in a sense, in unfamiliar territory. There was obviously a point that Monroe was keen to get across.

'Will this turbulence be difficult?' I questioned Monroe as our path increasingly sloped downwards.

'For some it will, yes. Those people who are ready and able to adapt should fare better. These adaptors will recognize that things cannot go on as they have been. There will be many who will question their lifestyles, their priorities, their goals, career choices, etc. In this respect I foresee that many people will be making important changes in their lives, perhaps even moving to different parts of the world – like you!' Monroe said, pointing his finger at me.

'Yes' I said with a nod. 'I did follow my own inner impulse in that regard. I had felt for some time that I needed to make some changes; to focus on what I felt I really needed to do.'

'And others will also follow their inner impulses in the times to come' added Monroe. 'It is important that people do not cling to their fears; now is the catalyst for change. In the words of one of your own ancient sayings: "A sign is enough for the alert, but a thousand counsels are not enough for the negligent".' Monroe grinned at me and shook his head. 'I love all these wise sayings you people have; shame so few of you take heed of them…oh well! Anyway, doing what is necessary may be very different from doing that which you want. It is good to remember that the importance of something in your world is often in inverse proportion to its attractiveness. That is why you have so many dinosaurs still roaming your beautiful planet.'

'What?! What do you mean we still have dinosaurs?' I exclaimed in an incredulous voice.

'Figuratively speaking my dear fellow, of course. All those people who will not change, or cannot change, are their own dinosaurs; and like your scaly predecessors they will meet their own extinction' Monroe said without a hint of emotion in his voice.

'You mean they will die early, prematurely, or they will eventually die a normal death and not be replaced….since the new generations are coming in?' I asked.

'Both in fact' answered Monroe as he stopped to scoop up a budding flower at the side of the path. 'The end result will be the same. The age of the dinosaur is past – the age of the phoenix is here.'

'Phoenix? Why is it the age of the phoenix?' Monroe did not reply immediately but instead walked over to me and placed the flower he had picked into one of my shirt button holes.

'It makes a pretty addition' he said smiling. 'It may not stay there for long; yet while it does it is at least an improvement' said Monroe with a straight face. 'I said the phoenix age' continued Monroe, 'as it signifies a new generation or configuration of human beings that will be rising as something new, from the ashes of something that is old. Dinosaurs do not rise, cleansed by fire, from the ashes. No sir, dinosaurs stomp around devouring…well, many of them did. Fire, too, signifies not only the purification process but also a lightness – it has an ethereal quality. This lighter, finer quality is coming to your planet, and to humanity; but not immediately. First, there will be some spring cleaning.' Monroe paused from speaking and tickled the ear of his little friend Fuko, who had been quietly scampering alongside us all the way.

'Spring cleaning?' I finally asked.

'Mmm...energetic cleansing. Yet the interference ripples will be there. And there will also be resistance from many terrestrial forces on this planet that do not wish to let go of their power and privileges.'

'You mean the rich people!' I said half-jokingly.

'The rich, in what you define as rich in your monetary terms, yes. But it is not about money. It is a question of power and control. And what is coming down the line – the recycling – will disrupt these power lines of control. And this will not be taken lightly. There is likely to be a mountain of confusion in your world before a meadow of spring. This, however it may appear, is necessary and part of the overall process. The hand of winter reveals the secrets of spring.'

Monroe smiled as he held out both his hands to me, palms down, then slowly turned them around. Within each palm lay what appeared to be a glistening stone, or rather what I would call a jewel. I could never be 100 percent sure as the sight lasted for such a brief moment. As suddenly as Monroe had revealed his hands then he clenched his fists and upon opening them again I saw they contained only two small pebbles, or ordinary rocks. 'From rough to smooth' said Monroe with a wink.

'Nice one' I said, a little sarcastically perhaps.

'A jewel in the mud is still a jewel – never forget this' said Monroe, eyeing me directly. 'Do not lose the precious centre. It is about integrity and self-respect. Self-respect costs nothing, and yet it gives the Earth. Whatever you have to deal with, do it with a willing heart. The coming years will be harsh to half-heartedness. Passion of the self is not about emotionality, nor intensity; it is about being genuine and fully present. Stop looking for enlightenment – first you need to become *fully human*. Now that is your goal!'

'And should it be everyone's goal also?' I asked, not sure if Monroe was talking to me or specifically about me.

'Everyone has their own mountain path to find; yet being fully human applies to each person that walks in a human body. Status is what society constructs around social roles and activities. A road cleaner can be more highly developed than a prince. Many great wisdom teachers in your past have gone unnoticed because of the natural disguise of social status. People are conditioned to overlook that which they are not expecting. You would be surprised to learn of how truth has been literally in front of your eyes all this time.'

'So being more fully human is also about seeing correctly, as well as inner balance and stability?'

'Being fully human' said Monroe with lucid voice and emphasis, 'is about clear perception and inner recognition. It is also about emotional, mental, and psychological balance. Being more than who we came here as is what we are here for. Only when we engage with our own development can a person begin to perceive beyond the false borders of a limited reality. Human self-development also aids and supports development upon other levels also; these levels you do not yet perceive, yet they are very real and very, very necessary. In other words, what I am trying to get across here – if you have not already figured this out' said Monroe with a flick of a glance toward me, 'is that evolution of the human being is a composite necessity. It is a necessity not only for each individual's well-being, but also as a necessary factor within a much grander picture. And that is part of what is already unfolding. You do not need to look surprised.' Monroe stopped walking and turned on the path to face me directly. 'You already know everything – all of you do. Yet it has been shielded from you. All the help we have given you, and all the assistance you have received from other quarters, has been to facilitate your access to your own awareness and records of the truth. A true guide works to make themselves obsolete.' Monroe turned away and continued walking down the sloping path. We both walked in silence for a while. My mind was preoccupied with its own thoughts.

We admired the craggy peaks that ascended on both sides of us; yet our path was straight. Vultures circled overhead, and glided on the uplifting currents of air. They may have been curious, yet there was no smell of death on these two men. Only, I hoped, the fragrance of life.

The path took us to the top ridge overlooking the town of Ubrique below.

'Now for the homeward stretch' said Monroe as he turned around and began walking back up the path.

'The same path back?' I called.

'The same path back' replied Monroe without turning around. I jogged to catch up with him. 'Only this time we are going uphill. Now this should be fun!'

'It seems that your traveling companion Fuko likes you' I said in an effort to make some pleasant and easy conversation.

'He has good instincts' was all Monroe said. The rest of our walk back was in silence. Often Monroe would turn to me and smile with a gentle squint of his eyes. In all our time together he had been nothing but friendly and gracious to me. I felt grateful to him, and also a little guilty that I had given, what I felt to be, so little in return. Yet I had never sensed any displeasure or bad feelings against me. On the contrary, Monroe had seemed more than pleased to be in my company on each occasion. I was fortunate, I felt, to be able to observe such impeccable behaviour.

After a further ninety minutes we were back at the first field where the Roman road began. Across from the road I could see my parked car. We had been walking for nearly three hours and I was now feeling a strong hunger and thirst.

'Time to celebrate our mini-marathon!' exclaimed Monroe without even a drop of sweat on his brow. Monroe strolled off up the road, with Fuko following. I lagged behind exhausted.

'Leading from behind?' asked Monroe cheerfully when I had finally caught up with him outside of a restaurant at the far edge of the small town of Benaocaz.

'Yes, it's my new foreign policy' I replied with a smile.

'Wonderful! Then let us go and colonize some rich pickings. I know you are going to like this food…even better than the last supper.' We entered the restaurant and took a small table in the corner by the window. Monroe asked for some water for Fuko and left his canine friend untied outside.

'Will he be okay? Won't he wander off?' I asked Monroe when he had returned.

'No, you don't need to worry – he's not human.'

I looked at the menu and my mouth began to water. It had a whole array of good local food. Before I could say anything two glasses of cold beer were placed on the table. Monroe and I looked at each other and smiled.

'Small pleasures, my friend' said Monroe and raised his glass.

'Salud amigo' I said as we clinked our glasses. Yes....cheers amigo.

I let Monroe select and order the food for the both us. I had no doubt as to his knowledge of local specialties and to his good taste. As we were high in the mountains the local dishes were meat based, and included a delicious plate of oven-cooked wild boar. I observed that whilst Monroe relished the food, he ate in a slow and delicate manner. I tried to follow his example, and as a result our lunch was not rushed but savored. We talked generally about my years of travel and some of my experiences in other cultures. Monroe listened attentively and, I felt, with great interest. At various intervals he would smile at something I said - an encounter or experience I recounted - or nod his head in agreement. For a while I had, literally, the whole table to myself. It was like two old friends sharing a warm meal together, with the many years that apparently separated our ages falling away into vapor.

When we had finished our food, and my storytelling had arrived at a long pause, Monroe gestured for the digital recorder to be placed on the table.

'I would like to add' said Monroe clearing his throat, 'that there are still some things to consider when you have the individual trying to evolve within society.' I listened and observed Monroe; not wishing to interrupt what was now his turn for storytelling. 'Society represents a community, which by its very nature makes certain assumptions about life, knowledge, and how a person can develop, if at all. A society, and the community, constitutes a stable entity so long as its basic assumptions are not questioned. This stability becomes a comfort zone for many, yet is liable also to inhibit progress. You see, these conditioned assumptions reinforce each other and creates a consensus of coherence, and therefore strength. This emotional stability is often highly valued by a majority of people. Such a social system, however, only serves to reinforce human dependency. The human picture of national and cultural history is the succession of social groupings based upon consensual ideologies and worldviews. It is more likely to provide assurance than opportunity for individual development. It is more often the case that people alter and "develop" their ideas to adjust to social and cultural formations – in other words, to fit in – rather than reshape their thinking patterns away from the support of the group. People often thus engage in their re-stabilization, alongside cultivated emotions of dissatisfaction, insecurity, and the need for "something else". Many societies have appropriated and cultivated this conversion-syndrome so that it operates through the individual themselves. Human civilization is often the history of dependency-oriented cultures, where the search for comfort and reassurance is built into the patterns of its function, often through artificially constructed methods. What we have noticed, and where we sometimes feel the need to be of assistance, is providing the information and/or the experiences necessary for people to break the attachments that are preventing them from contact with their genuine awareness and perception. Humans must learn to conceive of possibilities beyond their present state. Then they need to find the capacity within themselves to reach toward these possibilities. Often human societies and communities teach that what people need – their desires and goals – can be achieved through the framework of the system of which they are a part. The result of this is that each individual will only be able to achieve the results possible within the limited structure offered by that particular social system. The confusion, I would say, is that people neither sufficiently recognize this phenomenon, nor appreciate their own capacity for independent thought and development. This is a shame. Humanity needs to clear the mist from its collective eyes - you have existed for far too long within a fabric of myths, misunderstandings, and perplexity.' Monroe paused to order a glass of water.

'And do we need to clear this collective mist right now – is it time sensitive?' I asked.

'A lot will be cleared away in the years to come; I have already said this' Monroe stated calmly. 'Do not cling onto old beliefs or structures of thinking. Do not allow your societies to drag you into dependency emotions of fear, insecurity, and helplessness. A range of impacts will converge upon your planet over the coming years. Take these impacts to be opportunities for change and development, regardless of how they appear to be. And help others to change, adapt, and renew also. This time is yours now. We have let loose many chains and attachments you were not able to see. The future is truly yours to embrace and be a part of. Along with discomfort there are great waves of supportive energies coming your way. Take my word for it whether you "believe" me or not. Humanity will be part of a great future; I know because I have seen it' said Monroe smiling. 'The question that remains, however, is how well you ride yourselves through this change and how you deal with the necessities and potentials ahead. This part is in your hands, collectively and individually' Monroe said with a gesture of his open hands. 'I would like to say good luck, yet it is not a question of luck. So instead I shall say *good doings* and *good beings*!' I smiled and thanked Monroe as I rose from the table and made my excuse to leave.

On returning from the bathroom I saw Monroe standing at the bar chatting with a man who I presumed to be the owner. They were laughing together and obviously in good humor. When I approached Monroe lifted his hand and said, in what sounded like a perfect Spanish accent: *Aquí viene mi guía en Inglés*! Both men laughed as I smiled and returned a simple *Hola*. Monroe gestured to the door and suggested we hit the road. I collected my things from the table and we waved our amiable goodbyes and stepped outside into the mid-afternoon sunlight.
'Oh, what about paying!' I exclaimed once we were outside.
'It is my treat' said Monroe with a hand on my shoulder. 'After all, you listened wonderfully!'

I felt we were both in high buoyant moods after the good food and lunchtime ambience. With Fuko trotting at our side we walked down the road away from the restaurant. I had the sense we were not walking back in the direction of the car. I didn't say anything at first, trusting that Monroe knew exactly where we were heading. The clear blue sky hosted several birds gliding on the air currents above. We passed no-one on the road as we walked. Within a few minutes we arrived at a gate that lead onto a path that stretched away into the Grazalema mountains. Monroe turned to face me and looked deeply into my eyes with a warm smile.

'Well, another road starts here for me' he said, and looked off into the distance. I wasn't sure what he meant exactly, and just looked at him blankly. 'I will not be returning with you in the car – I never cared much for those noisy combustion engines on wheels!' he joked. We both laughed.

'So you are taking the high road then?' I asked, still not sure if he was being totally serious or not.

'Indeed I am my dear fellow' Monroe said and continued to look at me directly. Then it suddenly dawned on me.

'Ohhh…so you're heading off then?' I asked. Monroe let out a gentle chuckle.

'Yes, something like that. My road' Monroe said pointing toward the peaks, 'takes me into the mountains. And your road is, for now, back by car.' There was a moment of silence before Monroe added, 'it has been a great pleasure. I thank you for all your questions and good listening. And now it is *adios amigo*.' Monroe came forward and gave me a hug. 'Inspire yourself to move forward – and be an inspiration for others. Pass it along…' said Monroe as he clasped me by the shoulders. 'You have all the tools you need…within you. It is up to you to seek them and use them. And, as way of a companion, our little friend here will be staying with you…to keep a good eye on you!' Monroe smiled once more and turned to walk away.

'What is the greatest tool we have?' I quickly blurted out. Monroe turned as he closed the gate between us.

'It is the energy of genuine unconditional love, without fear or anger. You already know that.' Monroe, elegantly dressed as always, strode off on the mountain path without another look. I watched the figure in white disappear over the first hill, the sun shining high in the spring sky.

Fuko walked alongside me as we returned to where I had parked the car. My elation after the meal had now subsided into….into a sensation I had no words for. The drive home was one I shall never forget…nor could I ever forget.

AFTERWORD

IT took me several months to finally write up all the conversations into narrative chapters and to finish what I had started. I began to do this in the summer, once I felt more objective to the material. Fuko remains by my side, chasing birds and eating snails – and reminding me that Monroe was real and not a phantasm.

A couple of weeks after our final encounter in the high mountain town of Benaocaz I drove back to visit Benamahoma. My excuse was to buy some local honey. It was a familiar drive and brought back memories of those few weeks in Spring where I had delighted in these trips. Now, it almost seemed like a far memory.

After purchasing the jars of honey from a local seller I deliberately walked past the house where Monroe lived; or rather, where he had lived. It was no surprise to see both on the gate and door of the house the familiar sign stating *alquilar* – for rent. The energy and presence of the house was no more. It had moved on. I understood now what Monroe had meant when he said that truth exists according to the time, the place, and the people – and that none of these is static or forever. I felt gratitude for the special spring of 2012.

I have changed, and continue to change. The world continues to change too – and there are many more changes to come. Humanity did not come this far for nothing – we have all the tools we need within us. Now the journey really begins…

Kingsley L. Dennis, September 2012

Kingsley L. Dennis, PhD, is a sociologist, researcher, and writer. He is the author of several critically acclaimed books including *'The Phoenix Generation: A New Era of Connection, Compassion and Consciousness'* (2014); *'Breaking the Spell'* (2013); *'New Revolutions for a Small Planet'* (2012); *Struggle For Your Mind'* (2012); *'New Consciousness for a New World'* (2011); *'After the Car'* (2009 – with John Urry); and the celebrated *'Dawn of the Akashic Age'* (2013 - with Ervin Laszlo). Kingsley also publishes through his own imprint **Beautiful Traitor Books.** He previously worked in the Sociology Department at Lancaster University, UK. Kingsley is the author of numerous articles on social futures; technology and new media communications; global affairs; and conscious evolution. He currently lives in Andalusia, Spain.

For more information visit: **www.kingsleydennis.com**

Printed in Great Britain
by Amazon